Ways You Can Help

PicK One

The World
The Nation
Your Region
Your Community

Colin Ingram & Robert D. Reed

Robert D. Reed Publishers   •   Bandon, OR

Robert D. Reed Publishers
P.O. Box 1992
Bandon, OR 97411
Phone: 541-347-9882; Fax: -9883
E-mail: 4bobreed@msn.com
Website: www.rdrpublishers.com

Cover Designer: Cleone L. Reed
Book Designer: Amy Cole

ISBN 13: 978-1-934759-30-1
ISBN 10: 1-934759-30-9

Library of Congress Control Number: 2009902371

Manufactured, Typeset, and Printed in the
United States of America

Publisher's Note
All information presented in this book was accurate at the time of publication. For any changes that charities may have made, please see the individual organizations' current websites and other information sources as given in this book.

Contents

Introduction

On One Hand and On the Other

For most of us, every day in the mail we get a handful of solicitations from various organizations. Many of them have elaborate come-ons, alarming us with the news of some imminent catastrophe, showing us pictures of destitute or war-ravaged people, photos of endangered animals whose end is near, asking us to complete surveys, directing us to list our priority concerns—but always, always with a return form that asks for money. And there are the television pleas with photos of needy children or unwanted dogs with expressions so sad it breaks your heart to see them. And then…there are the telephone calls that often start with, "How are you, (using your first name as though you're a close friend) we want you to know we really appreciate your past support, and we know you won't want to miss the opportunity to…"

On the other hand: There are so very many needs in the world, so many tragedies, so much that needs doing. And it's not imaginary—it's real. And when you consider that most of what is going on is never reported, it's all overwhelming!

So what's a decent, caring person of conscience to do? Send in a donation to an organization whose effectiveness you're unsure of? Throw up your hands and say, "It's too much for me," and do nothing? It's hard to decide, and it's continuous because the solicitations keep coming and the real needs keep appearing.

Most of us would like to do more to help others who are less fortunate and to help make positive changes in the world. But these are the main obstacles: 1) We haven't any money or time to spare at all. Let's dispense with this first obstacle since there are very few of us who can't set aside even a little bit of money or time to help.

The intent of this book is to address the other obstacles, which are: 2) The needs are so vast that we're overwhelmed into numbness and inaction. 3) We're unsure whether or not a charity is legitimate and if our contributions really help. 4) We may feel deeply about a cause and want to help but we're unsure how to do it.

Why This Book and What We Learned

We began this book because, like you, we felt frustrated because we wanted to do more to help. In doing the extensive research that this book entailed, we learned a great deal. We can now say, unequivocally, that the number of people doing good things in every corner of this world is absolutely astounding!

There is the airborne, all-volunteer relief group of doctors, dentists and nurses who travel *at their own expense* to provide medical care in places where it is inaccessible. There is the organization that provides free housing at veterans' medical hospitals so that the families of severely wounded vets can stay close to them. There are the folks who come together to help endangered tribes reclaim the land that was stolen from them, and where the development projects for safe water and sustainable farming *are run entirely by indigenous people*. There is the terrific organization that enables donors to make small microloans *directly* to entrepreneurs to begin sustainable new businesses in impoverished villages—and 100% of the loan goes to the entrepreneur! And the dedicated staff of the organization that has saved literally tens of thousands of girls from female genital mutilation. And the list goes on and on.

Which Charities Are In This Book and Which Aren't

There are some 1.5 million registered charities in the U.S. Obviously we can only include a fraction of them in this book. What we have done is select those charities that we have researched and which have received high ratings by the major charity rating organizations. The major charity rating organizations are listed in the Resources section of this book. For each organization we have selected, we've given a description of what the organization does and how it uses the donations it receives and/or the volunteers it uses.*

Just because a charity isn't included here doesn't necessarily mean it is poorly run. There are several reasons why specific charities may have been omitted. First, there are simply too many of them, and many have overlapping or duplicated functions.

Where we have deliberately omitted a charity because of some flaw, the most common reasons are 1) too small a percentage of money is spent on actual services and too much is spent either on administrative costs or fundraising; 2) executives of the charity receive exorbitantly high salaries; 3) the programs of the charity have been found to be comparatively ineffective.

Yes, there are some venerable, well-known, well-established, prestigious charities that we have deliberately omitted because of one or more of the above flaws.

Another reason why a charity may have been omitted is because it is a sectarian organization that focuses its services on or favors a particular religious group. Yet several sectarian charities have been included where their services are intended for all persons regardless of religious affiliation.

And where the stated purpose of a charity is contentious, we have tried to include charities that are both for and against that purpose.

Of course, no organization is perfect. But the charities listed in this book have all been carefully vetted and found to be effective in their stated purpose and efficient in their use of money and/or volunteers.

* Exception: the purpose of charities dedicated to
specific diseases is obvious, and we have merely listed
but not described these organizations.

From the Charity's Point of View

When the managers of charities are asked what message they'd like to send to prospective donors, their answers are similar. One of the hardest things about running their operations is maintaining long-term projects when contributions are sporadic.

They'd like donors to make long-term commitments to giving, to support them through lean times as well as periods of plenty.

A way of looking at contributions to a charity is to view them as an investment. You are investing your money and/or time and you want some return on your investment. The best way to maximize your investment is steady, long-term support that will produce long term, sustainable change.

From the IRS's Point of View

Most charitable donations are tax deductible. To receive those deductions the IRS requires that you have proper documentation of your contributions. Most charities will send you a thank-you letter or a year-end statement for your contributions. While the IRS requires receipts for any contribution of $250 or more, it's a good idea to keep receipts of all your contributions. Canceled checks help but may not be acceptable to the IRS for all contributions. For non-cash donations of more than $500, you may need additional documentation such as IRS Form 8283.

Many charities have separated their lobbying activities from their educational activities by splitting into two legally separate organizations. Most often these are identified by their names. Example: The Nice Work charity and the Nice Work Foundation. Donations to the charity, itself, are not tax deductible while donations to the charity's foundation are deductible.

For more detailed information about charities and foundations, see the section on Definitions of Charities and Foundations.

When You Shouldn't Give

Avoid contributing to charities that:
1. Ask for cash donations.
2. Send you appeals that are in the guise of official looking government documents.

3. Describe their programs or services only in vague terms without any specifics of what their operations consist of.
4. Send you alarmist bulletins that describe an impending catastrophe when the facts indicate otherwise.
5. Threaten or pressure you in any way if you don't give.
6. Spend excessive amounts of money on management and/or fundraising. In this book we have provided information on how each charity uses financial contributions. In general, a charity should spend at least 75% of its expenses on the actual programs and services it provides. There are a few exceptions, such as when charities perform extensive lobbying activities that require large staffs and resultant high administrative expenses. In these cases, we have indicated why we've made an exception.

Volunteering

The United States is unique in all the world not only for the number of individuals that donate to charities, but for the incredible number of people who volunteer their time, energy, and skills. It is a fact that this nation could not survive in its present form without them.

Almost every charity has a volunteer program. Volunteers range from cooks to doctors, from athletic coaches to accountants, from mentors to meal deliverers, from disaster relief responders to language translators, and from blood bank assistants to construction helpers.

Some charities operate either mostly or solely with volunteers...hundreds of thousands of them in some cases. In the section on Ways to Volunteer, we've provided a good selection of them, including organizations whose sole purpose is to match prospective volunteers with opportunities.

When you talk to active volunteers, the majority of them will tell you that volunteering has been one of the finest experiences of their lives.

What You'll Find In This Book

We all have favorite causes, and you'll find no lack of them here. From promoting world peace, protecting animal rights, providing shelter for the homeless, promoting education, ensuring food safety, helping veterans, responding to disasters, promoting the performing arts, eliminating hunger, securing women's rights— and on and on.

We've listed the charities by categories so they're easy to locate. There's also an Index in the back of the book that lists the names of the charities and the pages on which they're found.

One Drop in the Ocean

You've probably heard of the very large U.S. foundations such as the Bill and Melinda Gates Foundation, the Ford Foundation, and the William and Flora Hewlett Foundation. They do wonderful things. So does Oprah's Angel Network. And on a massive scale there's the Clinton Global Initiative (CGI). Bill Clinton has gotten together 100 current and former heads of state, 14 Nobel Prize winners, major philanthropists, foundation heads, and leading CEOs to create a truly awesome charitable effort. CGI has now committed some $46 *billion* which will impact and dramatically improve the lives of more than 200 million people.

And then there's the smallest scale with the plant-a-seed factor. In Africa, a group of village women in a desperately poor area wanted to start a business baking bread for the local school but they had no oven. Across the world, an American woman in a small rural town read that the women had received microloans from several individuals, but lacked a final $25 donation to buy the oven. The American donated that $25 and the villagers got their oven.

The African ladies found that they could bake more than the local school needed. That prompted an enterprising local man to widen the dirt path to the next village so he could carry the ladies' extra bread on his bicycle. That proved successful enough that he was able to buy a new bicycle. That meant there was an unused bicycle in the village.

With profits from the bakery, the villagers were able to buy an inexpensive, bicycle-powered water pump, which saved all the village women a daily 6-mile, round-trip walk to the nearest well. Which meant they had more time to grow vegetables.

Then an international charity, working in the area, heard of their modest success. Instead of barging in with highly paid, foreign staff, the charity hired a dozen local women to see if it could be duplicated in the surrounding villages.

Well, the story continues, and it resulted in the majority of villages in a 200 square mile area being lifted out of poverty over a two-year period.

Which brings us back to the smallest scale and the plant-a-seed factor. One woman, who could spare $25, planted a seed which was the tipping point that changed the lives of several thousand villagers.

Final Thought

Yes, the needs of the world can seem overwhelming, but there are literally millions of creative, altruistic, strong, determined, competent people who are really—and we emphasize *really*—changing things. And they are doing it in every country, every corner of the globe, including in the United States of America.

So perhaps the most important message of this book is this: these good people working in every country are making a difference. So please don't give in to discouragement, to charitable numbness, or to cynicism that the problems are too great to solve. **PICK ONE** (or several). *You can make a difference.*

Does Community Service Really Change Anything?

by Raj Mundra

Raj Mundra is a teacher at the Phillips Academy in Andover, Massachusetts, assistant dean of the Office of Community and Multicultural Development, and founder and director of the Academy's Niswarth summer service-learning program. The following article describes the experience of the program's student/faculty trip to India to perform service, and what they learned about community, partnerships, and what really works.

Dust swirled as we trudged through the littered, stifling streets of Dharavi, in Mumbai (Bombay), India. Climbing a ladder to the windowless room that a family of six calls home, I thought: What does this impoverished community really get from our school's efforts at community service?

What long-term benefit does any underserved community truly derive from the Phillips Academy's—or any other organization's—outreach efforts? What differentiates well-intended programs to encourage global citizenship from those that seem more like "cultural tourism," and resume-building for high schoolers?

Phillips Academy high school students and faculty were toiling for Niswarth, a program where students go to Mumbai for three weeks to study urban development and serve in one of Asia's poorest areas. Niswarth is the Hindi translation of Philips' motto *non sibi* or "not for self." This year, Phillips students, partnered with Indian high schoolers and two nongovernmental organizations, were challenged to create a one-day project for this specific community. They were invited into shanties to practice the complex skill of observing without judgment. Everyone looks poor, but what is poverty? What are the root causes for almost 10 million people in Mumbai living in these conditions? What are the crucial social issues?

The answers to those questions are complex. And listening was crucial for participants. Students learned that residents were bulldozed out of their homes and moved to 225-sq.-ft. apartments in another part of the city. We went door-to-door, helping with an ongoing census and heard, "There is no school nearby." "We need to take three trains to get to our jobs." "We get clean water in our homes for only 20 minutes every three days." "We don't trust our neighbors here...."

Drawing on our studies on resource-poor communities and conversing with local students, we decided to address the need for clean water. Learning that India's new Right to Information Act mandates a timely response to citizen requests, and undeterred by India's infamous bureaucracy, students drafted a petition, got every resident of the seven-story building to sign it, and submitted it.

We also began cleaning the building using monsoon rainwater. Within 30 minutes into our effort, curiosity drew residents to see what our odd, intergenerational Indian/American group was doing.

Residents helped scrub, saying, "If you care about our living conditions we should take similar responsibility." Men, who rarely engaged in cleaning, participated by developing a pulley system to bring water buckets upstairs. Seeing this, residents of the adjacent building tackled their own hallways.

Spurred by our petition, the local warden informed over 25,000 residents that their home access to clean water would now be eight minutes every day—a considerable improvement over the 20 minutes available every three days.

Months later, this community has moved from distrust to action, addressing the quality of schools and access to medical facilities. A fundamental, sustainable transformation appears to be taking place. For all we took home from Mumbai, we have clearly left something of value.

Indian students asked about the biggest issue facing America. The answer is not recession, global warming, or healthcare, but how to engage young people to become change makers. We learned that it requires venturing outside comfort zones, listening to community needs, and sometimes partnering with local organizations. And that's what differentiates well-intended programs to encourage global citizenship from those that seem more like cultural tourism.

One participant said she came away from these three weeks "with a burning inspiration" to make change. Like others, she conveyed that she could no longer be content with simply standing on the sidelines.

Such reactions during this experience taught us that traditional community service is important, but has limited effect. Real results lay in understanding the larger issues, observing without judgment, practicing sophisticated empathy, and mobilizing the community to become partners in making fundamental changes are what have real effect on people's lives. And the key to raising generations of change makers in any community means combining services with learning, or "service-learning," in the years of adolescent idealism and energy.

What we have learned about engaging a foreign people in community service is that those who become part of the process are the ones who are truly served by community service. Long-term benefits for underserved communities lay in genuine partnerships that are based on mutual understanding. Students from America and residents in the slums of Mumbai were all out of their comfort zone during this program, and that is exactly the foundation that was required for real change to occur.

INTERNATIONAL CHARITIES

Pick One
How to Help Promote
World Peace

World Federalist Movement (WFM)

Federalism is the system of governance whereby various policy matters, by their nature, fall under the jurisdiction of international, national, or local governing bodies.

Created in 1947, WFM is an international organization founded on the belief that federalism at all levels must be strengthened in order to obtain lasting justice and peace in the world.

World Federalists call for the revamping of global and regional institutions to ensure collective peace, security, and development while retaining the legitimate sovereignty of nations. Recent examples of strengthened federalism on a regional level are the European and African Unions.

WFM has been a lead organization promoting the rule of law in world affairs, and it calls for the creation of an international legal system that prevents nations from going to war, settles disputes, and enforces treaties. WFM has been a key organization in establishing the International Criminal Court (ICC). One of its continuing purposes is to revamp the UN into a genuinely democratic institution whose charter enables it to legally prevent war and enforce peace. One aspect of this program is to establish a UN Emergency Peace Service as a rapidly deployable force.

WFM is recognized internationally for its expertise on matters of global governance, and it serves as the International Secretariat that informs and coordinates the activities of more than thirty other organizations devoted to promoting world peace and security.

World Federalist Movement (WFM), continued

WFM uses funding approximately as follows:
program expenses, 85%, administrative expenses, 9%,
fundraising expenses, 6%.
For further information:
Website: www.wfm.org
Address: 708 Third Ave, 24th Flr, New York,
   NY 10017
Telephone: 212-599-1320
Fax: 212-599-1332
Email: info@wfm.org

PICK ONE
HOW TO HELP PROMOTE
WORLD PEACE

The Carter Center (TCC)

TCC, founded by former President Jimmy Carter in 1982 in partnership with Emory University, works in 70+ countries to address a wide range of issues that are not covered by other organizations. In terms of promoting human rights it is widely known for its monitoring of elections, helping countries to build democratic institutions, preventing and resolving conflicts, and providing models for democratic governance.

Since 1989, TCC has sent teams of election observers to monitor more than 70 elections in 28 countries. It advises national governments on reform of campaign financing and provides models, plans, and best practices for democratic governance.

Although lacking any official authority from the U.S. government, TCC has become a trusted broker, serving as a channel for negotiations and dialogue in places of conflict. These areas have included Israel and Palestine, Sudan, Uganda, Haiti, Cuba, Egypt and Tunisia, to name a few.

TCC has convened international conferences that have brought together world leaders for securing and strengthening human rights. It has helped farmers greatly increase grain yields in 15 African countries. It has almost completely eliminated the scourge of Guinea Worm Disease and has played a leading role in the reduction of dozens of other diseases. And it has worked to eliminate the stigma of mental disease in many countries.

The center is guided by five main principles: It strongly emphasizes action and results; it avoids duplicating the efforts of other aid organizations; it accepts the possibility of failure by addressing difficult issues; it maintains strict neutrality in dispute resolution; and it believes that people can improve their lives when given the proper tools.

TCC has received numerous awards for its work. Among them, President Carter in 2002 received the Nobel Peace Prize for TCC's efforts "to find peaceful solutions to international conflicts, to advance democracy and human rights, and to promote economic and social development." In 2006, the Bill and Melinda Gates Foundation presented TCC with the Gates Award for Global Health.

The Carter Center uses funding approximately as follows: program expenses, 90.5.%, administrative expenses, 3.7%, fundraising expenses, 5.7%.
For more information:
Website: www.cartercenter.org
Address: 1 Copenhill, 453 Freedom Pkwy, Atlanta, GA 30307
Telephone: 800-550-3560
Email: carterweb@emory.edu

PICK ONE
HOW TO HELP PROMOTE
WORLD PEACE

Rotary International (RI)

Rotary International collaborates with the United Nations, governments, and nongovernmental organizations to improve the human condition throughout the world, advancing peace, health, education, and the alleviation of poverty.

RI's humanitarian programs fund health care, clean water, food, and other essential needs primarily in the developing world, and support a wide range of peace-enhancing programs. Among them are the Rotary Peace and Conflict Studies Program which provides professionals from around the world with the opportunity to be trained in conflict resolution and mediation strategies; the Rotary Friendship Exchange which helps Rotarians and their families to make reciprocal visits to other countries, staying in each other's homes, and learning about different cultures firsthand; the Rotary Youth Exchange which offers students the chance to travel abroad for cultural exchanges; the World Community Service which allows Rotary clubs from different countries to implement community service projects together; and grants are awarded to teachers to teach in developing countries.

Rotary International currently holds the highest consultative status offered to a nongovernmental organization by the UN's Economic and Social Council.

Rotary International (RI), continued

RI uses funding approximately as follows:
program expenses, 84%, administrative expenses, 5%,
fundraising expenses, 11%.
For further information:
Website: www.rotary.org
Address: 1560 Sherman Avenue, Evanston, IL 60201
Telephone: 847-866-3000
Email: contact.center@rotary.org

PICK ONE
HOW TO HELP PROMOTE
WORLD PEACE

AFS-USA (formerly American Field Service)

AFS is one of the oldest and largest cultural exchange organizations in the world, with student and teacher exchanges in some 65 different countries. It was founded in 1947 as the American Field Service and since then has provided exchange opportunities for some 375,000 students and teachers, with a current rate of 13,000 per year. High school students and grades K-12 teachers are eligible for exchange programs.

By providing international and intercultural learning experiences for individuals and families, the AFS mission is to help create a more just and peaceful world.

Volunteer hosts are an important part of this quest for greater understanding between different countries and cultures. Hosts offer a bed, meals, and for students, provide the same overall guidance that would be given to their own children. Hosts can be two- or one-parent families with or without children.

Exchange teachers are also an important part of the AFS program. A visiting foreign teacher can broaden and enrich curriculum by bringing different worldviews into the classroom.

Hosts are supported by local AFS staff from start to finish of the exchange period. Both hosts and guests find that their lives are enriched, a greater understanding of different cultures has been gained, language skills are improved, and lifelong connections are made.

The student and teacher exchange programs of AFS are made possible by host families, granting institutions, support of the U.S. State Department, individual donations, and by some 37,000 volunteers all over the world

AFS-USA, continued

AFS-USA uses funding approximately as follows: program expenses, 81%, administrative expenses, 11%, fundraising expenses, 8%.
For further information:
Website: www.afs.org/usa
Address: 71 West 23rd St, 17th Flr, New York, NY 10010
Telephone: 212-299-9000
Fax: 212-807-1001
Email: afsinfo@afs.org

PICK ONE
HOW TO PROMOTE ARMS
CONTROL WORLDWIDE

Union of Concerned Scientists (UCS)

What began as a collaboration between students and faculty members at the Massachusetts Institute of Technology in 1969 is now an alliance of more than 200,000 citizens and scientists. Among nonprofit organizations, UCS is arguably the most authoritative source for independent scientific analysis. Its staff is highly respected and is frequently called upon testify before government committees. Among its many accomplishments, UCS has taken a leading role in challenging the government's distortion and suppression of science.

It has provided landmark analyses of global warming, safety of genetically engineered crops, effects of invasive species, drug safety, renewable energy, etc. But it is perhaps best known for its work on nuclear weaponry and proliferation, and armament reduction in general. UCS was instrumental in helping to defeat funding for the Nuclear Earth Penetrator program; it was the lead organization in helping to legislate the moratorium on nuclear testing; it has taken a leading role in improving nuclear power plant safety; it has fought against space-based weaponry; and its analyses have been instrumental in demonstrating the ineffectiveness of missile defense systems.

Through its careful, unbiased science, UCS has helped to shape the legislative debate on the most important issues of our time, especially the reduction and eventual elimination of weapons of mass destruction.

Union of Concerned Scientists (UCS), continued

UCS uses funding as follows: program expenses, 80%, administrative expenses, 6%, fundraising expenses, 14%.
For further information:
Website: ucsusa.org
Address: 2 Brattle Square, Cambridge, MA 02238
Telephone: 617-547-5552
Fax: 617-864-9405
Email: giftinfo@ucsusa.org

PICK ONE
HOW TO PROMOTE ARMS
CONTROL WORLDWIDE

Ploughshares Fund

Ploughshares Fund is a public grantmaking foundation dedicated to preventing the spread and use of nuclear, biological, chemical, and other weapons of war, and preventing conflicts that could lead to the use of weapons of mass destruction. It is supported by donations from individuals and from other foundations.

Ploughshares Fund enables the smartest people with the best ideas for building a safer, more peaceful world to implement their ideas and achieve results. Since 1982, the organization has made grants totaling over $50 million to become the largest grantmaking foundation in the U.S. focusing exclusively on peace and security issues.

To reduce the threat from nuclear weapons, Ploughshares' grants focus on:

- Preventing new states from acquiring nuclear weapons
- Preventing both the accidental or intentional use of nuclear weapons
- Preventing the testing or development of new nuclear weapons by existing nuclear weapons states
- Reducing global stockpiles of nuclear weapons as steps toward the total abolition of nuclear weapons

To accomplish this and to help prevent the acquisition or use of all weapons of mass destruction and their delivery systems, Ploughshares provides grants for specific purposes to many organizations: Alliance for Nuclear Accountability, Arms Control Association, Bulletin of the Atomic Scientists and Campaign for a Nuclear Weapons Free World, Carnegie Endowment for International Peace, Center for Arms Control and Proliferation, and Federation of American Scientists.

Ploughshares Fund, continued

Ploughshares uses funding approximately as follows: program expenses, 83%, administrative expenses, 10%, fundraising expenses, 7%.
For further information:
Website: www.ploughshares.org
Address: Fort Mason Center, Bldg B, Suite 330,
    San Francisco, CA 94123
Telephone: 415-775-2244
Fax: 415-775-4529
Email: ploughshares@ploughshares.org

PICK ONE
HOW TO PROMOTE ARMS CONTROL WORLDWIDE

Center for Arms Control and Non-Proliferation (CACNP)

Established in 1980, CACNP is one of the leading organizations that does research, analysis, and public outreach on peace and security issues with a focus on weapons of mass destruction (WMDs). It has played an important role in informing policymakers on WMD issues.

CACNP carefully tracks Federal budget expenditures for defense and foreign policy and briefs Executive branch officials and Congress on national security issues. It coordinates with several other arms control and peacekeeping organizations to build consensus and support for sensible policies.

CACNP works to decrease the role of nuclear, chemical, and biological weapons in national security policy, reduce nuclear stockpiles worldwide, and maintain the moratorium on nuclear testing. It also works to strengthen the Nuclear Non-Proliferation Treaty (NPT) and to reduce all materials of potential WMD use that might become available to states and non-state groups.

CACNP uses funding approximately as follows: program expenses, 72%, administrative expenses, 16%, fundraising expenses, 12%.
For further information:
Website: www.armscontrolcenter.org
Address: 322 Fourth Street, NE,
     Washington, DC 20002
Telephone: 202-546-0795
Fax: 202-546-5142
Email. nhendrix@armscontrolcenter.org

PICK ONE
HOW TO PROMOTE HUMAN
RIGHTS WORLDWIDE

Amnesty International (AI)

AI's stated mission is to uphold the UN Universal Declaration of Human Rights. It is one of the most effective organizations in the world at publicizing and applying pressure against the holding of political prisoners and other prisoners of conscience, the abolition of torture, and other grave abuses of human rights.

AI maintains offices in 80 countries and operates in many more. It conducts research on human rights violations and acts to halt and prevent them by exerting influence on governments, international organizations, political groups, and businesses.

AI generates Urgent Action Appeals in multiple languages on behalf of individuals and groups that are at immediate risk, bringing these situations to the attention of millions.

Activist members publicize human rights offenses and mobilize action through lobbying, mass demonstrations, and vigils. The organization is active on a wide variety of issues, including opposing torture, freeing prisoners of conscience, protecting the rights of refugees and migrants, abolishing the death penalty, ending violence against women, and ending illegal arms trade.

AI maintains strict neutrality and objectivity. In the words of the organization, "We do not support or oppose any government or political system and neither do we necessarily support or oppose the views of the victims/survivors or human rights defenders whose rights we seek to protect."

Amnesty International (AI), continued

AI uses funding approximately as follows:
program expenses, 75.3%, administrative expenses,
2.8%, fundraising expenses, 21.9%.
For more information:
Website: www.amnesty.org
Address: 5 Penn Plaza, New York, NY 10001
Telephone: 212-807-8400
Fax: 212-627-1451
Email: aimember@aiusa.org

PICK ONE
HOW TO PROMOTE HUMAN
RIGHTS WORLDWIDE

Human Rights Watch (HRW)

This is the largest U.S. based organization that researches, reports on and combats inhumane conduct, discrimination, and other human rights abuses in every area of the world. At any given time HRW is active in some 70 countries.

The organization focuses on issues and places where attention is needed and where HRW can curtail current abuses and prevent future ones. HRW responds to emergencies but also combats longstanding, entrenched problems.

HRW reports and acts on a wide variety of human rights abuses, including in the areas of arms trade, children's rights, medical care access, terrorism and counterterrorism, justice, and refugee, ethnic minority and women's rights.

HRW researchers are frequently on-site in problem areas where they conduct field investigations, interview victims and witnesses, coordinate with local activists, journalist and lawyers, and seek contact with government officials.

HRW research is not just about victims and perpetrators; it involves finding out who has the influence and leverage to stop the abuse, and who should assume responsibility for redress.

HRW staff not only have a deep commitment to human rights, they are all seasoned experts in their countries and in the issues they focus on. When people read about, hear on the radio, or see on television some abuse that is occurring somewhere in the world, it is more than likely that the report comes from the diligence and global reach of HRW.

Human Rights Watch (HRW), continued

HRW uses funding approximately as follows:
program expenses, 76%, administrative expenses, 5%,
fundraising expenses, 19%.
For more information:
Website: www.hrw.org
Address: 350 5th Ave., 34th Fl., New York, NY 10118
Telephone: 212-290-4700
Fax: 212-736-1300
Email: hrwnyc@hrw.org

PICK ONE
HOW TO PROMOTE HUMAN
RIGHTS WORLDWIDE

Human Rights First (HRF)

HRF is an advocacy organization that focuses on human rights abuses in countries around the world from a legal perspective. Among the issues it addresses are international refugee policy, genocide intervention, combating hate crimes, ending torture, fighting discrimination, and prosecuting war crimes.

HRF advocates for change at the highest national and international policymaking levels. The organization is accorded Special Consultative Status to the United Nations and it frequently delivers reports to the UN Security Council as well as other international agencies and to national governments.

In the U.S. the organization has been active in a number of areas, including filing legal briefs in support of foreign nationals held by the U.S. without charges. And HRF developed a detailed plan for the new U.S. administration to end impunity for private security contractors in Iraq and elsewhere.

HRF is active in addressing rights abuses in several conflict zones, and has been especially active in lobbying governments and the UN to enforce existing sanctions against the Sudanese government over the appalling abuses in Darfur.

HRF has played an important role in the creation and launching of the Global Network Initiative, a new code of international freedom of expression that will take its place alongside the UN's Universal Declaration of Human Rights.

Human Rights First (HRF), continued

HRF uses funding approximately as follows: program expenses, 78.3%, administrative expenses, 11.2%, fundraising expenses, 10.4%.

When pro bono support from several law firms is included, HRF's percentage of total funding that goes to program expenses is increased to 94%.

For more information:

Website: www.humanrightsfirst.org

Address: 333 7th Ave., 13th Fl., New York, NY 10001

Telephone: 212-845-5200

Fax: 212-845-5299

Email: feedback@humanrightsfirst.org

PICK ONE
HOW TO PROMOTE HUMAN
RIGHTS WORLDWIDE

The Carter Center (TCC)

TCC, founded by former President Jimmy Carter in 1982 in partnership with Emory University, works in 70+ countries to address a wide range of issues that are not covered by other organizations. In terms of promoting human rights it is widely known for its monitoring of elections, helping countries to build democratic institutions, preventing and resolving conflicts, and providing models for democratic governance.

Since 1989, TCC has sent teams of election observers to monitor more than 70 elections in 28 countries. It advises national governments on reform of campaign financing and provides models, plans, and best practices for democratic governance. For more than twenty years, President and Mrs. Carter have personally intervened with heads of state on behalf of victims of human rights abuses and their defenders.

Although lacking any official authority from the U.S. government, TCC has become a trusted broker, serving as a channel for negotiations and dialogue in places of conflict. These areas have included Israel and Palestine, Sudan, Uganda, Haiti, Cuba, Egypt, and Tunisia, to name a few.

TCC has convened international conferences that have brought together world leaders for securing and strengthening human rights. It has helped farmers greatly increase grain yields in 15 African countries. It has almost completely eliminated the scourge of Guinea Worm Disease and has played a leading role in the reduction of dozens of other diseases. And it has worked to eliminate the stigma of mental disease in many countries.

The center is guided by five main principles: It strongly emphasizes action and results; it avoids duplicating the efforts of other aid organizations; it accepts the possibility of failure by addressing difficult issues; it maintains strict neutrality in dispute resolution; and it believes that people can improve their lives when given the proper tools.

TCC has received numerous awards for its work. Among them, President Carter in 2002 received the Nobel Peace Prize for TCC's efforts "to find peaceful solutions to international conflicts, to advance democracy and human rights, and to promote economic and social development." In 2006, the Bill and Melinda Gates Foundation presented TCC with the Gates Award for Global Health.

The Carter Center uses funding approximately as follows: program expenses, 90.5.%, administrative expenses, 3.7%, fundraising expenses, 5.7%.
For more information:
Website: www.cartercenter.org
Address: 1 Copenhill, 453 Freedom Pkwy., Atlanta, GA 30307
Telephone: 800-550-3560
Email: carterweb@emory.edu

Pick One
How to Promote Human
Rights Worldwide

Physicians for Human Rights (PHR)

Founded in 1986 by a group of doctors, PHR has become both an investigative and an advocacy organization for human rights all over the world. The U.S. Doctors, nurses, public health specialists, and scientists from PHR go to such places as disease-ravaged villages in the developing world, prisons in modern countries, as well as the offices of policymakers. Politicians, the courts, and the media use PHR as a reliable source of information due to their credibility and expertise.

In 1997 PHR was a co-recipient of the Nobel Prize for Peace as a founding member of International Campaign to Ban Landmines. The organization is a leading activist in efforts to end torture, an advocate for stronger international efforts to prevent genocide, and coordinator of public and private aid to treat HIV/AIDS. It mobilizes doctors who provide medical evidence for victims of persecution.

As well as testifying before the Congress, PHR staff have backpacked through deserts and toiled to uncover mass graves. The organization has received numerous awards for its groundbreaking work and for its disclosure of atrocities that would not otherwise have come to the attention of governments and the media.

Physicians for Human Rights (PHR), continued

PHR uses funding approximately as follows:
program expenses, 88%, administrative expenses, 6%,
fundraising expenses, 6%.
For further information:
Website: www.physiciansforhumanrights.org
Address: 2 Arrow St., Ste. 301, Cambridge,
    MA 02138
Telephone: 617-301-4211
Fax: 617-301-4250
Email: phrusa@phrusa.org

Pick One
How to Promote Human
Rights Worldwide

Enough Project (A project of the Center for American Progress, CAP)

Widespread crimes against humanity are rampant today in several areas of the world, and especially in Sudan, Chad, Somalia, Congo, and Uganda. The United States and the larger international community should long ago have responded to these travesties but inadequate attention, political will and action from our leaders have allowed them to persist.

The goal of the Enough Project is to create sufficient noise and action to halt ongoing atrocities and to prevent future ones.

To accomplish this, the Project is developing analyses of the causes, the policies and tools needed for change, a program of powerful advocacy, and a robust activism.

The Project will help social activists, student groups, business leaders, religious organizations, celebrities, and Diaspora networks make sure their outcries against these travesties are heard.

Practical policies to counter humanitarian crises will include promoting peace, protecting civilians, and punishing perpetrators.

All of these together—analysis, policies and tools, advocacy and activism—will be required not only to stop present atrocities but also to prevent future ones.

These problems can be solved. Much can be learned from countries such as Burundi, Liberia, Mozambique, Rwanda, Sierra Leone, and South Africa. These nations have successfully overcome crises and are now committed to creating peace, stability, and democracy.

It is past time to end the terrible humanitarian crises that persist. The Enough Project is a start.

Enough Project, continued

CAP uses funding approximately as follows:
program expenses, 92.5%, administrative expenses, 5%,
fundraising expenses, 2.5%.
For further information:
Website: www.enoughproject.org
Address: 1225 Eye St. NW, #307, Washington,
    DC 20005
Email: donate@americanprogress.org

PICK ONE
HOW TO HELP DISASTER
RELIEF WORLDWIDE

International Rescue Committee (IRC)

The history of the IRC goes back all the way to 1933, when Albert Einstein suggested that an organization was needed to assist Germans suffering under Hitler. Since then the IRC has provided disaster assistance around the world for more than seventy years. It has networks of first responders in 25 countries and is a recognized leader in emergency relief and resettlement for those affected by violent conflict or oppression. It mobilizes quickly and is typically one of the first organizations on the scene in major disasters, providing shelter, clean water, and healthcare as well as long-term services such as resettlement, rehabilitation, and education for refugees.

The IRC supports and provides assistance to refugees who have come to America. The organization advocates on behalf of all displaced people and fights for the safety and rights of vulnerable populations across the world.

IRC maintains close relations with the U.S. Agency for International Development (AID) and the Population, Migration, and Refugee Bureau of the U.S. State Department.

> IRC uses funding approximately as follows:
> program expenses, 90%, administrative expenses, 6%, fundraising expenses, 4%.
> For more information:
> Website: www.theirc.org
> Address: 122 E. 42nd St. New York, NY 10168
> Telephone: 877-733-8433
> Fax: 212-551-3180
> Email: fundraising@theirc.org

PICK ONE
HOW TO HELP DISASTER
RELIEF WORLDWIDE

Doctors Without Borders (DWB)

Also known as Médecins Sans Frontières, DWB began in 1971 as an international humanitarian organization created by French doctors and journalists.

Doctors Without Borders operates in some 60 countries and delivers emergency aid to those whose survival is threatened by natural disasters, armed conflict, epidemics, malnutrition, and those without access to medical care. The organization also runs hospitals, undertakes vaccination programs, and operates feeding centers for malnourished children.

DWB has been in the forefront of providing emergency medical care all over the world, and it does this with large numbers of highly skilled volunteers. DWB does not take sides or accede to the demands of governments or warring parties. DWB volunteers frequently work in the most remote or dangerous parts of the world. When crises unfold, they make themselves and their skills available on short notice, usually dedicating six to twelve months to each assignment.

The organization has earned a well-deserved reputation for providing care wherever it is needed, and DWB received the Nobel Peace Prize in 1999.

Doctors Without Borders (DWB), continued

DWB uses funding approximately as follows: program expenses, 84%, administrative expenses, 1%, fundraising expenses, 12%, and miscellaneous expenses (in-kind goods), 3%.

For more information:

Website: www.doctorswithoutborders.org

Address: 333 7th Avenue, 2nd Fl., New York, NY 10001

Telephone: 888-392-0392

Fax: 212-679-7016

Address for donations: Doctors Without Borders USA, P.O. Box 5030, Hagerstown, MD 21741

PICK ONE
HOW TO HELP DISASTER
RELIEF WORLDWIDE

Oxfam America

Oxfam America, the affiliate of Oxfam International, could be listed under any of a dozen charitable categories. In terms of disaster relief, it is one of the leading organizations that is pre-positioned on the scene when disasters occur anywhere in the world. In addition to short-term relief with medical, food, and shelter assistance, Oxfam follows up with solutions to minimize future casualties from natural disasters, conflicts, and other man-made disasters, and creates development projects to fight poverty, hunger, and injustice.

Oxfam operates in more than 120 countries. It has been a leading relief agency in the 2008 Myanmar cyclone, the 2008 China earthquake, the 2007 Bangladesh flood, the 2007 Peru earthquake, the continuing catastrophe of Darfur, the famine in Somalia, the 2006 Pakistan earthquake, the U.S. Katrina hurricane, and countless other disasters in the past.

In terms of Darfur alone, at the time of this publication Oxfam provides vital assistance to roughly 500,000 people: clean water, shelter, blankets, soap, disease prevention programs, and opportunities for a livelihood. Increased violence has made the work more treacherous and costly, but Oxfam is there for the long haul. Donations can be made to special relief efforts such as the Sudan Crisis Relief and Rehabilitation Fund.

Oxfam America, continued

Oxfam America uses funding approximately
as follows: program expenses, 79%, administrative
expenses, 5%, fundraising expenses, 16%.
For further information:
Website: www.oxfamamerica.org
Address: 226 Causeway St., 5th Fl., Boston,
    MA 02114
Telephone: 800-776-9326
Email: info@oxfamametrica.org

PICK ONE
HOW TO HELP ALLEVIATE
HUNGER WORLDWIDE

Save the Children Federation (SC)

SC, founded in 1932, is one of the leading organizations that provide comprehensive help to children all over the world with a major focus on alleviating hunger. SC operates in more than 50 countries and serves some 37 million children and 24 million adults who care for them.

Hunger in most of the developed world means the feeling we get if we skip a meal. But for millions of families around the world, hunger is a day-to-day, constant search just for survival. Chronic malnutrition, even at mild levels, increases susceptibility to many diseases and contributes to the deaths of 6.5 million children per year around the world. Chronic malnutrition of children under two often results in stunting—reduced height and permanently diminished physical and mental capacity.

The Food and Agriculture Organization of the United Nations estimates that over 840 million people—about one sixth of the population of the world's developing nations—are malnourished. Over 200 million of them are children. Save the Children distributes basic staples during times of crisis when food is in short supply.

Individual child and community sponsorships are available. Local field offices monitor and report on local services and progress to ensure that sponsored children are benefiting from these programs. Child sponsors annually receive updated information on their sponsored child, the current programs, projects in the child's community, and the challenges faced by those living in the community.

Save the Children Federation (SC), continued

SC uses funding approximately as follows:
program expenses, 90%, administrative expenses, 4%,
fundraising expenses, 6%.
For further information:
Website: www.savethechildren.org
Address: 54 Wilton Road, Westport, CT 06880
Telephone: 800-728-3843
Email: twebster@savechildren.org

PICK ONE
HOW TO HELP ALLEVIATE
HUNGER WORLDWIDE

Gleaning For The World (GFTW)

Founded in 1998, GFTW obtains and delivers surplus medical, food, and other critical supplies to humanitarian organizations throughout the world. GFTW does not have its own humanitarian projects. It provides expertise in international aid delivery and management, saving these non-governmental organizations (NGOs) significant sums. And it does this with extraordinary efficiency.

The average cost for NGOs to ship one 40-foot container of donated goods to their destinations is $35,000. They need to locate, store, sort, inventory, and ship supplies to people working in the field.

Using trained staff, proficient supply chains, and large numbers of volunteers, GFTW locates, sorts, inventories, and loads shipping containers *for less than 1% of the value of the supplies.* Donated supplies include medical and surgical goods, foods, shoes, and clothing.

Most companies dispose of excess stock by dumping it in landfills or incinerating it. GFTW obtains large amounts of in-kind donations because they save companies money by providing a low cost way to dispose of unwanted stock.

Thus GFTW saves corporations money, it saves NGOs money, and the poor gain much needed supplies. It does this with an efficiency that is one of the highest in the nonprofit world. *For every single dollar in private donations, GFTW is able to ship and deliver $72 worth of surplus supplies!* It has received the highest ratings from the major charity rating organizations.

Gleaning For The World (GFTW), continued

GFTW uses funding approximately as follows:
program expenses, 99.5%, administrative expenses,
0.5%, fundraising expenses, 0%.
For further information:
Website: www.gftw.org
Address: P.O. Box 645, Concord, VA 24538
Telephone: 877-913-9212
Email: info@gftw.org

PICK ONE
HOW TO HELP ALLEVIATE
HUNGER WORLDWIDE

Kids Against Hunger (KAH)

Founded in 1999, KAH packages and distributes specially developed, nutritionally complete food packages to hungry children in the U.S. and to starving children in developing countries.

The organization purchases raw ingredients that are specially formulated by food scientists to provide easily digested protein, carbohydrates, and vitamins necessary to prevent malnutrition and hunger-related diseases in children. The food packages are simple to prepare in that they require only boiling water to make a complete meal.

Since its inception, and with the help of more than 100,000 volunteers, KAH has sent some 50 million food meals to children in more than 40 countries, including a million meals sent to victims of Hurricane Katrina. Shipping is provided either by the U.S. Government or by international humanitarian organizations.

Volunteers package ingredients at the main facility in Minnesota and at some 30 independently run satellite facilities in 19 states and one in Canada. The entire network has the capacity to produce more than 20 million meals each year.

KAH takes special care to ship food packs only to places where the recipient organization is trusted to distribute it to needy children and not allow it to fall into the hands of corrupt officials. Also, KAH only ships food to places where and when it will not interfere with local food prices (such as drought areas where local food is unavailable).

And finally, KAH partners with recipient organizations that are committed to promoting local sustainability so that repeat distributions of emergency food are seldom necessary.

KAH receives funding from individual donors, corporations, foundations, churches, and synagogues. All satellite facilities are separate nonprofit organizations. KAH receives on-going support from an anonymous company for overhead so that some 90% of individual donations go directly toward the purchase of food.

KAH national uses funding approximately as follows: program expenses, 71%, administrative expenses, 14%, fundraising expenses, 15%.
For further information:
Website: www.feedingchildren.org
Address: 5401 Boone Avenue North, New Hope, MN 55428
Telephone: 866-654-0202
Email: info@kidsagainsthunger.com

PICK ONE
HOW TO HELP PROVIDE
HEALTH CARE
TO PEOPLE IN NEED

Doctors Without Borders (DWB)

Also known as Médecins Sans Frontières, DWB began in 1971 as an international humanitarian organization created by French doctors and journalists.

Doctors Without Borders operates in some 60 countries and delivers emergency aid to those whose survival is threatened by natural disasters, armed conflict, epidemics, malnutrition, and those without access to medical care. The organization also runs hospitals, undertakes vaccination programs, and operates feeding centers for malnourished children.

DWB has been in the forefront of providing emergency medical care all over the world, and it does this with large numbers of highly skilled volunteers. DWB does not take sides or accede to the demands of governments or warring parties. DWB volunteers frequently work in the most remote or dangerous parts of the world. When crises unfold, they make themselves and their skills available on short notice, usually dedicating six to twelve months to each assignment.

The organization has earned a well-deserved reputation for providing care wherever it is needed, and DWB received the Nobel Peace Prize in 1999.

Doctors Without Borders (DWB), continued

DWB uses funding approximately as follows:
program expenses, 84%, administrative expenses, 1%,
fundraising expenses, 12%, miscellaneous expenses
(in-kind goods), 3%.
For more information:
Website: www.doctorswithoutborders.org
Address: 333 Seventh Avenue, 2nd Floor, New York,
NY 10001
Telephone: 888-392-0392
Fax: 212-679-7016

PICK ONE
HOW TO HELP PROVIDE
HEALTH CARE
TO PEOPLE IN NEED

Mercy Ships (MS) (a sectarian organization)

MS has operated a fleet of hospital ships that have provided free medical in developing nations since 1978. The ships include state-of-the-art operating rooms and intensive care facilities. Volunteer crews from more than 30 nations serve onboard.

The organization has performed in excess of 30,000 surgeries (such as cleft lip and palate, cataract removal, facial reconstruction, crossed-eye correction, etc.), 180,000 dental treatments and has treated several hundred thousand people in village medical clinics. MS trains local health-care professionals in modern techniques and has taught some 100,000 people to perform primary health care.

In addition, MS has delivered in excess of $60 million of medical equipment and supplies. The organization also has completed hundreds of community projects, including water wells, schools, clinics, and orphanages in more than 70 nations.

More than 850 persons from some 40 nations serve as crews on the organization's ships, and more than 1600 short-term volunteers serve on the ships each year.

Mercy Ships is endorsed by such notables as George W. Bush, Tony Blair, Nelson Mandela, and the heads of state of Benin, Gambia and Liberia, to mention a few. In addition to private donations, MS receives in-kind contributions (medical and other support supplies) from such well-known corporations as Toyota, Microsoft, Alcoa, Canon, Johnson and Johnson, and Starbucks, and prominent NGO's such as Rotary International and Lions International.

NOTE: In addition to its healing and community support services, MS has an active Christian ministry program.

Mercy Ships (MS), continued

MS uses funding approximately as follows:
program expenses, 80.5%, administrative expenses,
9.5%, fundraising expenses, 10%.
For further information:
Website: www.mercyships.org
Address: PO Box 2020, Garden Valley, TX 75771
Telephone: 800-772-7447
Fax: 903-882-0336
Email: info@mercyships.org

Pick One
How to Help Provide
Health Care
to People in Need

Remote Area Medical Foundation (RAMF)

After years of research and planning, in 1985 founder Steve Brock created a vast, carefully developed network of men and women called the Remote Area Medical Volunteer Corps (RAMVC). These are volunteers who have come together to make a highly mobile, remarkably efficient, medical relief force. They include pilots, doctors, nurses, technicians, and veterinarians who go on expeditions *at their own expense* and treat hundreds of patients a day under some of the worst conditions in the world where medical treatment is often totally absent. The RAMVC provides free health care, dental care, eye care, and veterinary services.

This remarkable organization airlifts medical personnel and equipment to remote areas deemed to be in special need, operates an emergency air ambulance service, and has even parachuted medical personnel into difficult access areas. Locals are treated without any charge. So far, some 26,000 doctors, dentists, nurses, veterinarians, and medical support people have left the comfort of their homes and families to treat more than 300,000 patients. With RAMVC, all medical supplies, medicines, facilities, and vehicles are donated; and the entire operation functions on a tiny, shoestring budget that is almost unbelievable considering what is accomplished. RAMF is the nonprofit foundation that funds RAMVC.

Remote Area Medical Foundation (RAMF), continued

RAMF uses funding approximately as follows:
program expenses, 87%, administrative expenses,
11%, fundraising expenses, 2%.
For further information:
Website: www.ramusa.org
Address: 1834 Beech St., Knoxville, TN 37920
Telephone: 865-579-1530
Fax: 865-609-1876
Email: ram@ramusa.org

PICK ONE
HOW TO HELP PROVIDE
HEALTH CARE
TO PEOPLE IN NEED

Physicians for Peace (PP)

Founded in 1989, Physicians for Peace is an international organization that provides free clinical care, medical training, medical education, and donated medical supplies to areas that need it the most. PP sends teams of volunteer doctors, dentists, nurses, and physical therapists to Africa, Asia, South America, Middle East, Caribbean, and Eastern Europe.

The founding principle of PP is that those who desire to heal owe allegiance to no one country, ethnicity, or creed. The organization places emphasis on promoting peace by uniting medical volunteers from opposing sides of conflicts and from diverse cultures. PP has created successful teams from Palestine and Israel, Iraq and Iran, Turkey and Greece, and the Philippines and Japan.

Physicians for Peace do everything from fitting prosthetics, treating burns, correcting clubfeet and cleft palates, to open-heart surgery-in places where these services have never been available before.

Each team remains in a specific area for one to six weeks and in addition to providing care, the teams train local medical professionals in the most up-to-date practices, drugs, and equipment.

Physicians for Peace (PP), continued

PP runs a very efficient operation, as these expense figures show: program expenses, 97%, administrative expenses, 2%, fundraising expenses, 1%.
For further information:
Website: www.physiciansforpeace.org
Address: 229 West Bute St., Suite 200, Norfolk, VA 23510
Telephone: 757-625-7569
Fax: 757-625-7680
Email: donate@physiciansforpeace.org

PICK ONE
HOW TO HELP PROVIDE
HEALTH CARE
TO PEOPLE IN NEED

Gleaning For The World (GFTW)

Founded in 1998, GFTW obtains and delivers surplus medical, food, and other critical supplies to humanitarian organizations throughout the world. GFTW does not have its own humanitarian projects. It provides expertise in international aid delivery and management, saving these non-governmental organizations (NGOs) significant sums. And it does this with extraordinary efficiency.

The average cost for NGOs to ship one 40-foot container of donated goods to their destinations is $35,000. They need to locate, store, sort, inventory, and ship supplies to people working in the field.

Using trained staff, proficient supply chains and large numbers of volunteers, GFTW locates, sorts, inventories, and loads shipping containers *for less than 1% of the value of the supplies.* Donated supplies include medical and surgical goods, foods, shoes, and clothing.

Most companies dispose of excess stock by dumping it in landfills or incinerating it. GFTW obtains large amounts of in-kind donations because they save companies money by providing a low cost way to dispose of unwanted stock.

Thus GFTW saves corporations money, it saves NGOs money, and the poor gain much needed supplies. It does this with an efficiency that is one of the highest in the nonprofit world.

For every single dollar in private donations, GFTW is able to ship and deliver $72 worth of surplus supplies!

It has received the highest ratings from the major charity rating organizations.

Gleaning For The World (GFTW), continued

GFTW uses funding approximately as follows: program expenses, 99.5%, administrative expenses, 0.5%, fundraising expenses, 0%.
For further information:
Website: www.gftw.org
Address: P.O. Box 645, Concord, VA 24538
Telephone: 877-913-9212
Email: info@gftw.org

PICK ONE
HOW TO HELP PROVIDE
HEALTH CARE
TO PEOPLE IN NEED

Rotary Foundation (RF) of Rotary International

Rotary International collaborates with the United Nations, governments, and nongovernmental organizations to improve the human condition throughout the world. The mission of the Rotary Foundation (RF) is to support Rotary International in advancing peace, health, education, and the alleviation of poverty. The Foundation's humanitarian programs fund health care, clean water, food, and other essential needs primarily in the developing world.

An example of Rotary's collaborations is its flagship program, PolioPlus, which works with UNICEF, the U.S. Centers for Disease Control and Prevention, and the World Health Organization to eradicate polio worldwide. RF has contributed over $600 million and its 1.2 million members have provided countless volunteer hours to help immunize more than two billion children against this disease.

Rotary currently holds the highest consultative status offered to a nongovernmental organization by the UN's Economic and Social Council.

RF uses funding approximately as follows: program expenses, 84%, administrative expenses, 5%, fundraising expenses, 11%.
For further information:
Website: www.rotary.org
Address: 1560 Sherman Avenue, Evanston, IL 60201
Telephone: 847-866-3000
Email: contact.center@rotary.org

Pick One
How to Help Eliminate
Poverty Worldwide

CARE USA

Founded in 1945, the organization's original name stood for "Cooperative for American Remittances to Europe." These were the familiar CARE packages that were sent to European survivors of World War II. In later years, as CARE's coverage broadened, the full name was changed to "Cooperative for Assistance and Relief Everywhere," and that is a fair description of what the organization does.

Because of its breadth, CARE could be listed under any of a dozen charitable headings. It is listed under the poverty heading because it focuses on empowering women, with the belief that women have the power to help whole families and communities escape poverty.

This is a very large and very effective organization. With 12,000+ staff who are mostly locals, it has directly helped some 65 million people in 71 countries. It currently oversees about 800 poverty-fighting programs in Africa, Asia, Eastern Europe, Latin America, and the Middle East. These programs improve education, prevent the spread of HIV and other diseases, increase access to safe water and sanitation, improve nutrition, expand economic opportunity and protect natural resources, to name a few.

CARE USA is supported by a combination of individual donations, corporations, foundations, and government agencies.

CARE USA, continued

> CARE uses funding as follows: program expenses,
> 91%, administrative and miscellaneous expenses, 5%,
> fund raising expenses, 4%.
> For further information:
> Website: www.careusa.org
> Address: 151 Ellis Street, NE, Atlanta, GA 30303
> Telephone: 404-681-2552
> Email: info@care.org

PICK ONE
HOW TO HELP ELIMINATE
POVERTY WORLDWIDE

ActionAid International USA (AAI)

AAI was formed in 1972 and has been one of the leading international anti-poverty agencies. Its vision is to help create a world without poverty and injustice in which every person enjoys their right to a life with dignity

Since its inception it has aided some 13 million people in 42 countries, helping them gain rights to adequate food, shelter, work, education, and healthcare.

AAI's concept is to work with local communities to determine best solutions. It then coordinates with regional, national, and international organizations to bring together the best skills and abilities and enable them to be used efficiently. Partnering with more than 2000 other organizations worldwide, AAI works to influence local, regional, and national governments to improve and strengthen their policies toward eliminating poverty and improving rights for the poorest of their citizens, and to provide a voice in the decisions that affect their lives.

AAI uses funding approximately as follows:
program expenses, 90%, administrative expenses, 8%, fundraising expenses, 2%
For further information:
Website: www.actionaid.org
Address: 1420 K Street NW, Suite 900, Washington, D.C. 20005
Telephone: 202-835-1240
Fax: 202-835-1244
Email: courtney.spellacy@actionaid.org

PICK ONE
HOW TO HELP ELIMINATE
POVERTY WORLDWIDE

Oxfam America

Founded in 1970, Oxfam America is one of the leading anti-poverty organizations. It works to end global poverty through saving lives, strengthening communities, and campaigning for change. In more than 120 countries, Oxfam is on the scene, helping people gain the hope, skills, and direction to create a new future.

The goal in all of Oxfam's anti-poverty programs is to enable poor people to exercise their right to manage their own lives. This includes collaborating with local partner organizations to enable impoverished people to make a decent, sustainable living. Oxfam provides assistance and expertise for protecting local natural resources, creating peace and security in the region, establishing equality for women, promoting indigenous and minority rights, and securing long-term, environmentally sound global trade.

The organization is very active in engaging with the public, government, private sector, and the international community. It produces a variety of research reports and educational materials on issues relating to poverty and international development, many of which are used to raise public awareness. Through its work and its education programs, Oxfam exerts a significant influence on the U.S. Congress and other government entities to support development efforts.

Oxfam America, continued

Oxfam America uses funding approximately as
follows: program expenses, 79%, administrative
expenses, 5%, fundraising expenses, 16%.
For further information:
Website: www.oxfamamerica.org
Address: 226 Causeway Street, 5th Floor, Boston,
    MA 02114
Telephone: 800-776-9326
Email: info@oxfamametrica.org

PICK ONE
HOW TO PROVIDE SHELTER
FOR FAMILIES IN NEED

Habitat for Humanity International (HFHI)

(a sectarian organization)

Several organizations provide temporary shelter after natural disasters and other emergencies. HFHI International is one of the very few major organizations that creates permanent housing in countries around the world.

Founded in 1976, HFHI is a nonprofit organization whose goal is decent shelter for everyone, worldwide. The organization utilizes volunteers plus donations of money and materials to build or rehabilitate houses with the help of partner families. The houses are sold to partner families at no profit, and the monthly mortgage payments are used to build more Habitat houses. Houses are based upon need regardless of background, race, or religion.

Habitat houses are not given free. An affordable down payment and mortgage payments are required. The houses are sold to partner families at no profit, and the families invest hundreds of hours building their own houses and also help to build other Habitat houses. The cost of Habitat houses ranges from $800 in some developing countries to an average $60,000 in the U.S.

Selection of families is based on three criteria: level of need, willingness and ability to contribute sweat equity, and ability to repay the loan.

HFHI works through independent, locally run affiliates that direct all aspects of home building, including fundraising, family selection, site selection, construction, and the servicing of mortgages. Local affiliates are asked to give 10% of their received donations for house building in other countries.

HFHI has built more than 300,000 homes in countries around the world, providing decent housing for some 1.5 million people.

Habitat for Humanity International (HFHI), continued

HFHI uses funding approximately as follows: program expenses, 81%, administrative expenses, 4%, fundraising expenses, 15%.
For further information:
Website: www.habitat.org
Address: 121 Habitat Street, Americus, GA 31709
Telephone: 800-422-4828
Email: publicinfo@habitat.org

PICK ONE
HOW TO PROVIDE SHELTER
FOR FAMILIES IN NEED

CHF International (CHFI)

Founded in 1952 and formerly known as the Cooperative Housing Foundation, CHFI is one of the largest providers of services to the developing world. The organization delivers a wide range of services each year to more than 20 million people in some 30 countries. CHFI provides services in agriculture, health, education, the environment, disaster relief, etc. And in particular, more than 115,000 beneficiaries have received new homes or shelter improvements in areas of disaster or environmental emergency. In addition to homes for the displaced or impoverished, new schools and health clinics are built. To date, the organization has made some $47 million in microloans available for housing and small businesses.

CHFI works with local people to determine the actual needs of a community. It then employs local labor, uses local materials, and creates solutions that best suit the needs of the community or region. CHFI has developed a solid reputation for engaging with and involving communities in a way that keeps decisions, ownership, and control of land and resources in their own hands.

Examples of CHFI programs are the slum community projects in India and Ghana, where the urban poor for the first time are having a meaningful voice in the planning and development of improvements in their communities. Here, as in many developing countries around the world, inadequate housing is tied to problems of water, sanitation, and transportation. These CHFI programs are resulting in close coordination among local governments, academic institutions, micro-finance banks, and other non-governmental organizations so that local services support not only the construction of new housing, but also the ability of the owners to properly maintain it.

CHF International (CHFI), continued

CHFI uses funding approximately as follows:
program expenses, 92.5%, administrative expenses,
6%, fundraising expenses, 1.5%
For further information:
Website: www.chfinternational.org
Address: 87601 Georgia Ave., Silver Spring,
    MD 20910
Telephone: 301-587-4700
Fax: 301-587-7315

PICK ONE
HOW TO HELP CHILDREN
IN DEVELOPING COUNTRIES

Save the Children Federation (SC)

SC, founded in 1932, is one of the leading organizations that provide comprehensive help to children all over the world. Their programs focus on a wide range of assistance, including health, hunger, literacy, protection from violence, and disaster relief. SC operates in more than 50 countries and serves some 37 million children and 24 million adults who care for them. Those involved include parents, community members, local organizations, and government agencies.

Education programs emphasize basic learning, both formal and informal, that help children and adults develop reading, writing, and mathematics skills. SC's health programs focus on the survival, health, and development of women and children, emphasizing child survival, reproductive health (including family planning, safe motherhood, and HIV/STD prevention), and nutrition.

Individual child and community sponsorships are available. Local field offices monitor and report on local services and progress to ensure that sponsored children are benefiting from these programs. Child sponsors annually receive updated information on their sponsored child, the current programs, projects in the child's community, and the challenges faced by those living in the community.

SC uses funding approximately as follows:
program expenses, 90%, administrative expenses, 4%,
fundraising expenses, 6%.
For further information:
Website: www.savethechildren.org
Address: 54 Wilton Road, Westport, CT 06880
Telephone: 800-728-3843
Email: twebster@savechildren.org

PICK ONE
HOW TO HELP CHILDREN
IN DEVELOPING COUNTRIES

The Smile Train

This organization focuses exclusively on correcting cleft lip and palate in children (cleft palate is an opening in the roof of the mouth). It currently operates in 71 developing countries and coordinates thousands of "partners" in those countries.

In addition to being shunned and prevented from attending school, many children with cleft lip and/or palate cannot speak or eat properly. An estimated 3.4 million children need surgery to correct these conditions. The Smile Train has developed techniques to correct these conditions that require only a single surgery of an hour or less, for a cost of only $250 per child, the lowest cost anywhere for corrective surgery of this type.

What a difference this surgery makes in creating a normal life for a child!

The Smile Train is unique among major charities in that 100% of donations go directly to programs. This is made possible due to the fact that board members pay all administrative, overhead, and fundraising expenses. Donations of any amounts are acceptable. Here is what is accomplished for a given donation: $25 covers sutures for one surgery; $50 provides medications for one surgery; $250 provides cleft surgery for one child.

The Smile Train, continued

The Smile Train uses funding approximately as follows: program expenses, 80%, administrative expenses, 1%, fundraising expenses, 19%.
For more information:
Website: www.smiletrain.org
Address: 245 5th Avenue, Ste. 2201, New York, NY 10016
Telephone: 877-543-7645
Email: info@smiletrain.org

Pick One
How to Help Children
in Developing Countries

Kiwanis International Foundation (KIF)

KIF was created to assist Kiwanis International in serving the children of the world. Despite worldwide advances in the awareness of children's problems and increasing efforts to solve them, children are still suffering from hunger, abuse, neglect, and improper or substandard medical care.

Kiwanis International (KI) currently has a membership of more than 600,000 men, women, and children in some 16,000 clubs in more than 70 countries and geographical areas. Members of these clubs volunteer millions of hours of their time in communities around the world.

As an example of their achievements, in 1994 KI launched its first Worldwide Service Project in partnership with UNICEF to eliminate iodine deficiency disorders (IDD). To date, IDD projects have been funded in 95 nations and KIF has raised nearly $100 million to eliminate this deficiency worldwide.

In addition to its many health care programs for children, KI, through guidance and example, works to develop future generations of leaders. Every day, Kiwanian volunteers are revitalizing neighborhoods, organizing youth-sports programs, tutoring, building playgrounds, and performing countless other projects to help children and communities.

KI maintains the highest standards of ethics and morals to create the high idealism that makes possible the increase of righteousness, justice, patriotism, and goodwill in countries through out the world.

Kiwanis International Foundation (KIF), continued

KIF, the foundation that supports KI, uses funding approximately as follows: program expenses, 82%, administrative expenses, 4%, fundraising expenses, 14%.

For further information:

Website: www.kiwanis.org

Address: 3636 Woodview Trace, Indianapolis, IN 46268

Telephone: 800-549-2647

Fax: 317-471-8323

Email: foundation@kiwanis.org

PICK ONE
HOW TO PROMOTE WOMEN'S
RIGHTS WORLDWIDE

Americans for UNFPA (AUNFPA)

UNFPA stands for United Nations Fund for Population Activities, and AUNFPA is a nonpartisan, nonprofit U.S. organization that builds support for and actively promotes this UN program.

UNFPA's mission is to "…promote the right of every woman, man, and child to enjoy a life of health and equal opportunity. UNFPA supports countries in using population data for policies and programs to reduce poverty and to ensure that every pregnancy is wanted, every birth is safe, every young person is free of HIV/AIDS, and every girl and woman is treated with dignity and respect."

Americans for UNFPA, AUNFPA, is dedicated to building American support for the work of UNFPA and to restoring the United States' moral, political, and financial contribution to the organization.

Reproductive health conditions are the leading cause of death and illness in women of childbearing age worldwide. Every minute, a woman in the developing world dies from treatable complications of pregnancy or childbirth, and for every woman who dies as many as 20 others are seriously injured by childbearing.

- UNFPA's stated goals include:
- Universal access to reproductive health services by 2015
- Universal primary education and closing gender gap in education
- Reducing maternal mortality by 75 per cent by
- Reducing infant mortality
- Universal access to accurate information, a range of safe and affordable contraceptive methods, and sensitive counseling
- Ensuring that quality obstetric and antenatal care is available to all pregnant women

For more than 30 years UNFPA has been a leader in the promotion of gender equality and is the largest organization devoted to assisting women, supporting legal and policy reforms that empower women worldwide.

AUNFPA uses funding approximately as follows: program expenses, 69%, administrative expenses, 14%, fundraising expenses, 17%.
For further information:
Website: www.americansforunfpa.org
Address: 370 Lexington Ave., Suite 702, New York, NY 10017
Telephone: 646-649-9100
Fax: 646-649-9139
Email: info@americansforunfpa.org

PICK ONE
HOW TO PROMOTE WOMEN'S
RIGHTS WORLDWIDE

Global Fund for Women (GFW)

GFW is an international network that advocates for women's human rights by making grants to support women's groups around the world. The organization makes grants to seed, strengthen, and link women's groups outside the U.S. Grants are based on the belief that women, themselves, know best how to determine their needs and how to propose solutions to existing conditions.

Grants include issues such as ensuring economic opportunity, ending gender-based violence and discrimination, ensuring adequate health care, advancing reproductive rights, gaining access to education, and expanding social and political participation.

Most grants range from $500 to a maximum of $20,000 and focus on lasting rather than short-term change. Grant proposals are accepted in any language and in any format.

GFW receives some 3000 proposals each year and is able to fund about 500. An expert advisory council of more than 100, plus input from past and current grantees, provides advice to the Board of Directors. The Board, which makes final grant decisions, consists of women leaders from all over the world.

Focusing on five geographic regions—Africa, Latin America and Caribbean, Asia and Oceania, Eastern Europe, Middle East, and North Africa—GFW has granted in excess of $65 million to some 3600 women's organizations in 167 countries. The organization has made significant advances in women's rights in each of these regions.

Global Fund for Women (GFW), continued

GFW uses funding approximately as follows:
program expenses, 79%, administrative expenses, 7%,
fundraising expenses, 14%.
For further information:
Website: www.globalfundforwomen.org
Address: 1375 Sutter St., # 400, San Francisco,
    CA 94109
Telephone: 415-202-7640
Fax: 415-202-8604
Email: donations@globalfundforwomen

Pick One
How to Promote Women's
Rights Worldwide

Center for Reproductive Rights (CRR)

CRR is a leading legal advocacy organization that defends women's reproductive rights by using international human rights law to advance the reproductive freedom of women. It works with more than 100 organizations in 45 nations, including Africa, Asia, East Central Europe, and Latin America and the Caribbean.

CRR believes reproductive freedom is one of the basic tenets of human dignity, self-determination, and equality embodied in the UN's Universal Declaration of Human Rights. And that the Universal Declaration of Human Rights needs strong law that will, in the end, determine if women are free to decide whether and when to have children; whether they will have access to contraception, health care, abortion, and safe pregnancy care; and whether they will be able to make reproduction choices without coercion.

CRR has worked across the world to improve the right to a private doctor-patient relationship; the elimination of harmful practices such as female genital mutilation; access to reproductive health care for women facing economic or social barriers; and protecting reproductive health workers from violence and coercion.

CRR uses funding approximately as follows:
program expenses, 77%, administrative expenses, 8%, fundraising expenses, 15%.
For further information:
Website: www.reproductiverights.org
Address: 120 Wall St., 14th Flr., New York, NY 10005
Telephone: 917-637-3671
Fax: 917-637-3666
Email: contribute@reprorights.org

PICK ONE
HOW TO PROMOTE WOMEN'S
RIGHTS WORLDWIDE

Tahirih Justice Center (TJC)

TJC was founded in 1997 to provide legal services for refugee and immigrant women who have fled to the U.S. after having undergone human rights abuses. The TJC is named after a 19th century woman of the Bahai faith who fought for the freedom and equality of women in Persia and was martyred for her then-radical views.

TJC has provided direct legal, social, and medical services for some 6000 abused women. To serve the ever-increasing number of women in need, TJC makes extensive use of volunteer attorneys, doctors, nurses, and social service professionals. Their public advocacy and their fight to establish women's rights resulted in legal victories that set a national precedent and revolutionized asylum law in the United States.

The efficiency and effectiveness of this organization was recognized by winning the 2007 Washington Post Award for Excellence in Nonprofit Management.

TJC uses funding approximately as follows: program expenses, 94%, administrative expenses, 3%, fundraising expenses, 3%.

For further information:

Website: www.tahirih.org

Address: 6066 Leesburg Pike, #220, Falls Church, VA 22041

Telephone: 703-575-0070

Fax: 703-575-0069

Email: justice@tahirih.org

PICK ONE
HOW TO HELP PROTECT
THE ENVIRONMENT WORLDWIDE

The Nature Conservancy (TNC)

TNC is probably the largest conservation organization in the world. Its stated purpose is: "to preserve the plants, animals and natural communities that represent the diversity of life on Earth by protecting the lands and waters they need to survive."

TNC addresses threats to natural land and marine ecosystems from development, fire, climate change, invasive species, overgrazing, unsustainable farming, etc. It accomplishes this by purchases, exchanges, partnerships, management agreements, and conservation easements.

Since 1951 more than 117 million acres of land and 5,000 miles of rivers have been protected worldwide. TNC has been involved in everything from grasslands to coral reefs, and it currently operates more than 100 marine conservation projects. With more than one million members, the organization works in all 50 states and in more than 30 countries.

The key to all of these successful conservation projects is applying sound science with market-based solutions and partnering with government agencies, businesses, international institutions, and other nonprofit organizations.

TNC has developed a strategic planning process called *Conservation by Design*, which identifies the highest priority landscapes, and seascapes that need protection—places that have the best chance of ensuring continuing biodiversity. The organization's goal is no less than securing the future of the natural world.

The Nature Conservancy (TNC), continued

TNC uses funding approximately as follows:
program expenses, 80%, administrative expenses,
12%, fundraising expenses, 8%.
For further information:
Website: www.nature.org
Address: 4245 N Fairfax Drive, #100, Arlington,
VA 22203
Telephone: 800-628-6860
Email: membership@tnc.org

PICK ONE
HOW TO HELP PROTECT
THE ENVIRONMENT WORLDWIDE

Natural Resources Defense Council (NRDC)

Founded in 1970, NRDC has become one of the nation's most effective environmental action groups, combining the grassroots power of 1.2 million members and online activists with the courtroom clout and expertise of more than 350 lawyers, scientists, and other professionals. Its purpose is to safeguard the Earth, its people, its plants and animals, and the natural systems on which all life depends. Because NRDC operates both in the U.S. and abroad, it is listed here and in the category of Environmentalism for the Nation.

NRDC works to solve the most pressing environmental issues we face today, including curbing global warming, getting toxic chemicals out of the environment, moving America beyond oil, reviving our oceans, saving wildlife and wild places, and helping China go green. Programs include teaming up with corporations to promote energy efficiency and environmentally responsible production practices, protecting forests and endangered ecosystems from development, and encouraging natural resource protection through the expansion of wildlife and marine reserves.

NRDC strives to protect nature in ways that advance the long-term welfare of present and future generations but also to foster the fundamental right of all people to have a voice in decisions that affect their environment.

Worth Magazine has named NRDC one of America's 100 best charities and *The New York Times* calls it "One of the nation's most powerful environmental groups."

Natural Resources Defense Council (NRDC), continued

NRDC uses funding as follows: program expenses, 80%, administrative expenses, 8%, fund raising expenses, 12%.

For further information:

Website: www.nrdc.org

Address: 40 West 20th Street, New York, NY 10011

Telephone: 212-727-2700

Fax: 212-727-1773

Email: membership@nrdc.org

PICK ONE
HOW TO HELP PROTECT
THE ENVIRONMENT WORLDWIDE

Worldwatch Institute (WI)

WI is a research organization that provides analysis of critical global issues, including climate change, resource sustainability, population growth, and poverty. For more than three decades, WI has been a primary source of information for governments around the world, business leaders, and academics. The organization uses innovative strategies for dealing with these issues by carefully researching their underlying causes and developing innovative solutions such as needed legislation, creative investments and, on an individual level, changes in lifestyles.

WI's programs include developing sustainable farming methods, creating a system to dramatically reduce the use of fossil fuels, and building an overall, sustainable global economy. The organization is noted as one of the premier sources for environmental information. It disseminates its research to more than 150 partner organizations and governments in 40 countries, and it provides continuing reports on all of these issues for the media.

WI uses funding approximately as follows:
program expenses, 78%, administrative expenses, 9%, fundraising expenses, 13%.
For further information:
Website: www.worldwatch.org
Address: 1776 Massachusetts Avenue, NW,
 Washington, DC 20036
Telephone: 202-452-1999
Fax: 202-296-7365
Email: worldwatch@worldwatch.org

PICK ONE
HOW TO HELP PROTECT
THE ENVIRONMENT WORLDWIDE

Conservation International (CI)

CI is one of the leading conservation organizations whose mission is to preserve global diversity and to demonstrate that human societies can successfully co-exist with this diversity. CI works in countries around the world, including in remote and sometimes dangerous places that may not be accessible to other groups. The organization is often the first to set foot in remote areas and, as a consequence, it is at the forefront of discovering new species or those thought to be extinct.

With networks of scientists, CI conducts some of the most ambitious and comprehensive assessments of ecosystems, utilizing everything from the most sophisticated satellite imagery to on-site, on-your-knees sampling. These assessments help identify those wilderness and seascape areas that are most in need of urgent action plans.

One of the goals of CI is to fill remaining knowledge gaps on a global basis, and to use the latest technologies to anticipate trends. This helps to pinpoint endangered areas and species before their conditions become critical. This pioneering research is then shared with other environmental organizations to better respond to emerging threats.

In addition to its extensive research team, CI helps indigenous people care for their lands by helping local communities design systems for sustainable agriculture and hunting, and by providing financial support until they are established on their own.

CI also partners with businesses, including Wal-Mart, Starbucks, and McDonald's, to help them establish practices that use natural resources in the most efficient and sustainable ways.

Conservation International (CI), continued

CI uses funding approximately as follows:
program expenses, 85%, administrative expenses,
11%, fundraising expenses, 4%.
For further information:
Website: www.conservation.org
Address: 2011 Crystal Dr, Suite 500, Arlington,
    VA 22202
Telephone: 800-429-5660
Fax: 703-892-1862
Email: inquiry@conservation.org

PICK ONE
HOW TO HELP PROTECT
THE ENVIRONMENT WORLDWIDE

Rocky Mountain Institute (RMI)

Established in 1982, Rocky Mountain Institute is an applied research organization that advises governments, businesses, communities, and individuals on the efficient and sustainable use of natural resources. It does this through the focus on Natural Capitalism, a new and rapidly spreading business model that harnesses sound environmental performance as an engine of competitive advantage. Natural Capitalism shows these kinds of groups how to create more wealth and employment by doing what they do more efficiently.

RMI has created ideas and models that have reframed the debates on climate change, energy production, transportation, and water usage, to name a few. The organization has developed pioneering strategies for self-sustaining communities, clean energy systems based on hydrogen, and new engineering and architectural techniques that dramatically improve the human, environmental, and financial performance of buildings.

In all its work, RMI is independent and non-adversarial, with a strong emphasis on market-based solutions that at the same time sustain and restore a healthy environment.

Rocky Mountain Institute (RMI), continued

RMI uses funding as follows: program expenses, 73%, administrative expenses, 19%, fundraising expenses, 8%.

For further information:

Website: www.rmi.org

Address: 2317 Snowmass Creek Rd., Snowmass, CO 81654

Telephone: 970-927-3851

Fax: 970-927-4510

Email: outreach@rmi.org

PICK ONE
HOW TO HELP PROTECT
THE ENVIRONMENT WORLDWIDE

Rainforest Alliance (RA)

Founded in 1987, the goal of RA is to conserve biodiversity and encourage sustainable livelihoods by making farming, forestry, and tourism environmentally sound and economically productive. The organization currently operates in more than 60 countries, seeking to transform land use practices, business practices and consumer behavior.

RA works with everyone from large, multinational corporations to small, community cooperatives to set standards that bring responsibly produced products to market. The organization sets standards that conserve natural ecosystems and wildlife and that promote economic progress and the welfare of workers and their communities. Farms and forestry businesses that meet these standards receive the Rainforest Alliance Certified™ seal. RA also works with tourism enterprises to succeed while leaving the lowest footprint on the local environment.

The Rainforest Alliance also operates several other programs, including: For teachers, lessons, presentations, stories and articles, etc., that help connect students to conservation. The Eco-Exchange program offers reporters, other conservation groups, foundations, and government agencies news about the latest environmental issues and successful projects. There are also a number of programs whereby donors can choose to help specific areas and projects.

Rainforest Alliance (RA), continued

RA uses funding approximately as follows:
program expenses, 93%, administrative expenses, 2%,
fundraising expenses, 5%.
For further information:
Website: www.rainforest-alliance.org
Address: 665 Broadway, #500, New York, NY 10012
Telephone: 888-693-2784
Fax: 212-677-2187
Email: development@ra.org

PICK ONE
HOW TO HELP PROTECT
THE ENVIRONMENT WORLDWIDE

Greenpeace

Greenpeace is an independent, global organization with some 2.8 million supporters worldwide and activities in 40 countries. Its aims are to work for disarmament and world peace; create an energy revolution to mitigate climate change; protect the world's oceans and forests; campaign for sustainable agriculture; and eliminate hazardous chemicals in manufacturing and in products.

Greenpeace exists to expose governments and corporations when they fail to safeguard our environment, our health, and our security. The organization has a history of "bearing witness" in a non-violent manner. Examples of this are the Greenpeace ships that expose illegal ocean dumping of toxic wastes; that interrupt fishing vessels engaged in destructive bottom trawling; and that attempt to stop pseudo-scientific whaling.

The purpose of these high-profile activities is to bring critical issues to the public's attention and to raise public debate. Through its activities, Greenpeace has enabled literally millions of citizens in countries around the world to take actions in support of the environment. In addition to high-profile activities, Greenpeace does research, lobbying, and quiet diplomacy.

One of Greenpeace's unique strengths stems from its ability to conduct campaigns that transcend national borders. By undertaking complex negotiations with international forums and corporations it has been able to challenge environmental threats and promote positive changes.

The organization has a long record of successes, including forcing safer standards in nuclear power plants; forcing the closure of toxic-spewing, coal-burning plants; ending illegal logging in several countries; lobbying governments to outlaw toxic PVC in toys; stopping the inclusion of dangerous chemicals in electronics products; helping enact safety restrictions on genetically-modified foods, and so on.

Donations to Greenpeace are not tax-deductible. Donations to the Greenpeace Fund (GF), its educational, tax-exempt affiliate, are tax-deductible.

Greenpeace uses funding approximately as follows: program expenses, 78%, administrative expenses, 3%, fundraising expenses, 19%. For Greenpeace Fund, figures are: program expenses, 80%, administrative expenses, 5.5%, fundraising expenses, 14.5%. For further information on Greenpeace:
Website: www.greenpeace.org/usa
Address: 702 H Street NW, Washington, DC 20001
Telephone: 800-328-0678
Email: info@wdc.greenpeace.org

PICK ONE
HOW TO PROMOTE RENEWABLE ENERGY WORLDWIDE

Worldwatch Institute (WI)

WI is a research organization that provides analysis of critical global issues, including climate change, resource sustainability, population growth, and poverty. For more than three decades, WI has been a primary source of information for governments around the world, business leaders, and academics. The organization uses innovative strategies for dealing with these issues by carefully researching their underlying causes and developing innovative solutions such as needed legislation, creative investments, and, on an individual level, changes in lifestyles.

WI's programs include developing sustainable farming methods, creating a system to dramatically reduce the use of fossil fuels, and building an overall, sustainable global economy. The organization is noted as one of the premier sources for environmental information. It disseminates its research to more than 150 partner organizations and governments in 40 countries, and it provides continuing reports on all of these issues for the media.

WI uses funding approximately as follows:
program expenses, 78%, administrative expenses, 9%, fundraising expenses, 13%.
For further information:
Website: www.worldwatch.org
Address: 1776 Massachusetts Avenue, NW,
    Washington, DC 20036
Telephone: 202)-452-1999
Fax: 202-296-7365
Email: worldwatch@worldwatch.org

Pick One
How to Promote Renewable
Energy Worldwide

Center for Resource Solutions (CRS)

Founded in 1997, the goal of CRS was to provide the necessary leadership to increase the demand and use of renewable energy around the world. Now, although CRS is a relatively small organization, it has a big impact. It creates innovative environmental policies and consumer protection mechanisms for renewable energy, energy efficiency, and greenhouse gas reductions that are used nationally and around the world.

CRS sponsors international meetings between energy policy-makers around the world. It has an important role, in cooperation with Australia, Canada, Mexico, and the International Energy Agency (IEA), in developing global energy policies. CRS has been a key player in helping to create China's Sustainable Energy Program.

Through its *Green-e* logo, CRS has created the leading voluntary program in the U.S. that certifies that renewable energy projects meet sound environmental standards. The organization's *Green-e Climate* program certifies that greenhouse gas reduction projects (offsets) are legitimate. The *Green-e Marketplace* logo establishes that businesses and other organizations have achieved renewable energy excellence.

Overall, CRS has been a major contributor to the development and use of renewable energy throughout the world.

In addition to individual donations, CRS is partially supported by the U.S. Department of Energy, the Environmental Protection Agency, the National Park Service, as well as many corporations and foundations.

Center for Resource Solutions (CRS), continued

CRS uses funding approximately as follows:
program expenses, 78%, administrative expenses,
18%, fundraising expenses, 4%.
For further information:
Website: www.resource-solutions.org
Mail Address: PO Box 29512, San Francisco,
    CA 94129
Headquarters Address: Presidio Bldg, Arguello at
    Moraga, San Francisco, CA 94129
Telephone: 415-561-2100
Fax: 415-561-2105
Email: info@resource-solutions.org

PICK ONE
HOW TO PROMOTE RENEWABLE
ENERGY WORLDWIDE

Solar Electric Light Fund (SELF)

For more than 18 years, SELF has provided renewable energy to villages in undeveloped countries all over the world. SELF's mission is to provide solar power and wireless communications to a quarter of the world's population living in energy poverty.

The organization's work includes all aspects of setting up renewable energy systems in communities. SELF develops projects with full local participation. It designs renewable systems, locates micro-financing, procures equipment, trains technicians, manages system installation, provides spare parts, and develops plans for long-term system sustainability.

In addition to villages and individual households, SELF brings solar power to clinics, schools and public facilities. Large numbers of solar drinking water systems have been installed. The health of thousands of people has been transformed by bringing a sustainable source of electricity to health centers.

SELF is currently bringing solar-powered Internet communications to thousands of students. The organization has partnered with SolarNetOne on continent-wide collaborative projects to bring wireless Internet access to impoverished areas that do not have a reliable power or a communications grid.

In agriculture, the organization focuses on solar-powered irrigation systems. All projects are based on self-help, self-reliance, and self-determination. Projects are chosen by local people; they are purchased by villagers through micro-credit financing, and each family pays for its individual system and is part-owner of cooperative community systems; and both men and women are trained to install, maintain, and replicate their solar systems for the benefit of others.

A partial list of SELF's past partners includes Columbia and

Stanford Universities, the World Bank, the United Nations, U.S. Department of Energy, and Habitat for Humanity.

> SELF uses funding approximately as follows:
> program expenses, 86%, administrative expenses, 7%,
> fundraising expenses, 7%.
> For further information:
> Website: www.self.org
> Address: 1612 K Street, NW #402, Washington,
>   DC 20006
> Telephone: 202-234-7265
> Email: info@self.org

PICK ONE
HOW TO CREATE ENTREPRENEURS
IN DEVELOPING COUNTRIES

ACCION International

Founded in 1961, ACCION provides microloans and business training to poor men and women who start their own businesses. In tandem with 30 partner lending organizations in 23 countries, ACCION has disbursed $9.4 billion over the last decade to help people work their own way up the economic ladder with dignity and pride. In 2005, ACCION and its partners provided loans to over 1.8 million poor entrepreneurs. Their goal is to bring microfinance to tens of millions of people—enough to truly change the world.

ACCION provides technical assistance, equity financing, and loan guarantees to local organizations which enables them to serve the poor while meeting their bottom lines and thriving as lending institutions.

These microfinance programs have the potential to cover their own costs. The interest each borrower pays helps to finance the cost of lending to another. In most poverty alleviation efforts, every person helped brings the program closer to its financial limits. Successful microfinance programs, on the other hand, generate more resources with each individual they help. ACCION's historical repayment rate has been 97 percent.

The organization has received numerous awards and grants for its work (such as from the Gates Foundation), and Worth Magazine has named it among the 100 best charities in the U.S., chosen from over 800,000 nonprofit organizations.

ACCION International, continued

ACCION uses funding approximately as follows: program expenses, 77%, administrative expenses, 13%, fundraising expenses, 10%.
For further information:
Website: www.accion.org
Address: 56 Roland Street, #300, Boston, MA 02129
Telephone: 617-625-7080
Fax: 617-625-7020
Email: donate@accion.org

PICK ONE
HOW TO CREATE ENTREPRENEURS
IN DEVELOPING COUNTRIES

International Development Enterprises (IDE)

IDE is a unique, international non-profit organization that has been helping poor farmers in developing countries escape poverty for more than 25 years. IDE works with small farmers to identify and develop appropriate technologies that increase productivity, generate cash income, and/or improve quality of life for the rural poor. IDE currently operates in Bangladesh, Cambodia, Ethiopia, Myanmar, Nepal, Vietnam, Zambia, and Zimbabwe

This organization has pioneered a market-based approach that has enabled millions to *permanently* escape poverty. It uses business principles to enable the rural poor to participate effectively as micro-entrepreneurs and earn income. To aid the development of these technologies (such as inexpensive drip irrigation systems and foot-operated water pumps), IDE trains and equips local small-scale enterprises to manufacture, distribute, install, and service the technologies at a fair market price. In this way, their programs create an environment that helps small farmers progress from subsistence agriculture to commercial farming, beginning an upward spiral out of chronic deprivation and vulnerability.

In IDE programs, the concepts and practices associated with private business are applied to the problem of poverty, such as:

- Identify market opportunities that can be exploited by poor people
- Develop technologies that the poor can use to generate income
- Establish supply chains to deliver technologies to the poor at affordable prices
- Establish linkages with output markets
- Ensure that everyone in the market network, especially the smallholder, receives a fair profit

IDE has received numerous grants for its work from major foundations around the world (including the Gates Foundation).

IDE uses funding approximately as follows: program expenses, 83%, administrative expenses, 11%, fundraising expenses, 6%.
For further information:
Website: ide-international.org
Address: 10403 W Colfax, #500, Lakewood,
    CO 80215
Telephone: 303-232-4336
Fax: 303-232-8346
Email: info@ideorg.org

PICK ONE
HOW TO CREATE ENTREPRENEURS
IN DEVELOPING COUNTRIES

Kiva (Kiva means "unity" in Swahili)

Kiva is the world's first person-to-person micro-lending website, empowering individuals to lend directly to entrepreneurs in the developing world. Lenders can choose one or more individual entrepreneurs to lend to. Kiva then passes the funds to one of their microfinance partners in the selected country, and that microfinance partner distributes the loan to the entrepreneur. *100% of each loan goes to the entrepreneur.*

The microloans help a real person make great strides towards economic independence and improve life for themselves, their family, and their community.

The minimum loan is $25. The schedule for repayment of loans is usually 6-12 months, at which time the lender receives his/her money back or can re-loan to other entrepreneurs.

Kiva channels all loans through local micro-lending partners because they are experts in choosing qualified entrepreneurs, and because they are in the best position to monitor the loans and provide any necessary training or other support to maximize the entrepreneur's chance of success.

It is possible (from disease, crop failure, etc.) for an entrepreneur to default on a loan and a lender to lose his/her money. However, this is a rare occurrence; the current repayment rate is 99.71%, and the Field Partner looks at a variety of factors (past loan history, village or group reputation, feasibility of business idea, etc.) before deeming the entrepreneur as credit worthy.

Kiva operates in 42 countries. It currently has 285,000 lenders who, collectively, have made 43,000 loans.

In addition to individual donors, Kiva has won the support of Microsoft, Google, Yahoo, You Tube, Facebook, Advanta Bank Corp, PayPal, and Starbucks.

Kiva, continued

For further information:
Website: www.kiva.org
Address: 3180 18th St., San Francisco, CA 94110
Telephone: 415-641-5482
Email: (email via website)

PICK ONE
HOW TO CREATE ENTREPRENEURS
IN DEVELOPING COUNTRIES

Heifer Project International (HPI)

Founded in 1944, HPI is a humanitarian assistance organization that provides income-producing livestock, training, and agricultural resources to impoverished families around the world.

Recipients are trained in animal care and sound agricultural practices so they can lift themselves out of poverty and become self-reliant. Milk, eggs, wool, meat, draft power, and other benefits of animals provide nutrition, and their sale provides money for education, housing, health care, and small business enterprises.

Benefits of every donated animal are multiplied because all recipients must agree to pass on some of their animal offspring and training to other needy families.

HPI's sustainable approach has been characterized by long-term development, rather than short-term relief. By donating one or more of their animal's offspring to another family in need, project sustainability is ensured, the community gradually becomes more self-sufficient, and each donor's self-esteem is enhanced by allowing recipients, themselves, to become donors.

Donors can choose from a wide variety of gifts to a family, including heifers, sheep, goats, chickens, ducks, geese, honeybees, etc.

Since its inception, HPI has helped seven million families in more than 125 countries improve their quality of life and move toward greater self-reliance.

Heifer Project International (HPI), continued

It uses funding approximately as follows: program
expenses, 75%, administrative expenses, 7%,
fundraising expenses, 18%.
For further information :
Website: www.heifer.org
Address: One World Avenue, Little Rock, AR 72202
Telephone: 800-422-0474

PICK ONE
HOW TO CREATE ENTREPRENEURS
IN DEVELOPING COUNTRIES

Opportunity International (OI)

Founded in 1971, the goal of OI is to end poverty in the developing world by helping to start small businesses and strengthening communities among the poor. It does this by what is called *microenterprise.* This began with microcredit (provision of very small loans) and grew to include additional services such as business training, savings education, insurance programs, and community cooperatives.

OI saw that the weak economies of the developing world could not create jobs without helping poor entrepreneurs create their own businesses. In addition, they realized that the developed world needed to change how it viewed the poor. Rather than being viewed as victims, OI realized that the poor, themselves, are the key to their emergence from poverty. James D. Wolfensohn, President of the World Bank, put it in these words, "We will not solve the problem of poverty or global peace or stability unless we change our perception of poor people from the object of charity to the asset on which you build a better world."

The world's poorest people are good credit risks. A lifetime of struggling for mere survival creates the kind of drive necessary to build a small business. In addition, OI creates Trust Groups, where 15-40 entrepreneurs guarantee each other's loans and act as a support network. Loan repayment rates exceed 98%.

Currently, OI consists of 42 branches in 28 developing countries. They serve in excess of a million active clients worldwide and have loaned more than seven million dollars. Their goal is to serve 100 million poor people by year 2015.

Opportunity International (OI), continued

OI uses funding approximately as follows:
program expenses, 87%, administrative expenses, 3%,
fundraising expenses, 10%.
For further information:
Website: www.opportunity.org
Address: 2122 York Road, #150, Oak Brook,
    IL 60523
Telephone: 800-793-9455
Fax: 630-645-1458
Email: getinfo@opportuity.org

PICK ONE
HOW TO PROMOTE SUSTAINABLE
POPULATION LEVELS WORLDWIDE

Americans for UNFPA (AUNFPA)

UNFPA stands for United Nations Fund for Population Activities, and AUNFPA is the U.S. organization that builds support for this UN program.

UNFPA's stated mission is to "...promote the right of every woman, man, and child to enjoy a life of health and equal opportunity. UNFPA supports countries in using population data for policies and programs to reduce poverty and to ensure that every pregnancy is wanted, every birth is safe, every young person is free of HIV/AIDS, and every girl and woman is treated with dignity and respect."

UNFPA seeks to improve the lives of individuals by informing them and offering more reproductive choices that can alter existing population trends.

In 1994, at the International Conference on Population and Development in Cairo, Egypt, 179 countries agreed that reproductive education and health is a prerequisite for poverty reduction and sustainable development. Included in this program was the goal of providing universal reproductive health services by year 2015. UNFPA is a key part of reaching this goal by providing its expertise on reproductive health and population issues.

At the request of individual countries, UNFPA provides education on a range of safe and affordable contraceptive methods, counseling, pre-and post-natal care, and the prevention and management of sexually transmitted diseases.

Reproductive health supplies are crucial to the success of UNFPA's programs. To this end, the organization plays a key role by forecasting needs in countries and regions, mobilizing donors to provide needed items, and coordinating the entire process.

UNFPA works in some 150 countries and territories.

Americans for UNFPA plays a key role in helping to support this highly effective UN agency. While AUNFPA receives support from corporations and foundations, the majority of its support comes from individual contributions.

AUNFPA uses funding approximately as follows: program expenses, 69%, administrative expenses, 14%, fundraising expenses, 17%.
For further information:
Website: www.americansforunfpa.org
Address: 370 Lexington Avenue, Suite 702,
    New York, NY 10017
Telephone: 646-649-9100
Fax: 646-649-9139
Email: info@smericansforunfpa.org

PICK ONE
HOW TO PROMOTE SUSTAINABLE
POPULATION LEVELS WORLDWIDE

Population Action International (PAI)

PAI is an independent advocacy group that seeks to inform policymakers of the linkages between population levels, reproductive health, the environment, and economic development. Founded in 1965, PAI helps to preserve global resources and improve individual well-being by mobilizing political and financial support for family planning and sound reproductive health policies.

PAI develops evidence-based reports on the impact of population change on the environment and its implications for human security and sustainable economic development. In the United States, the organization coordinates with policymakers to strengthen, fund, and implement programs. It is one of the leading creators and sponsors of conferences, meetings, and seminars on sustainable population levels.

PAI also partners with other similar non-governmental organizations in countries around the world by providing them with technical and financial assistance. PAI also monitors UN agencies, the World Bank, and other multilateral organizations to assess progress in the areas of sustainable population levels and reproductive health programs.

Behind everything that PAI does is the belief that every person has a right and access to sexual and reproductive health, so that humanity and the natural environment can exist in balance and fewer people live in poverty.

Population Action International (PAI), continued

PAI uses funding approximately as follows:
program expenses, 79%, administrative expenses,
11%, fundraising expenses, 10%.
For further information:
Website: www.populationaction.org
Address: 1300 Nineteenth Street, NW, Suite 200,
 Washington, DC 20036
Telephone: 202-557-3400
Email: pai@popact.org

PICK ONE
HOW TO PROMOTE SUSTAINABLE
POPULATION LEVELS WORLDWIDE

Population Media Center (PMC)

PMC addresses the issues of AIDS avoidance, the benefits of smaller families, and gender equality in developing countries around the world. It does this by what is termed the Whole Society Strategy. In each country where it is active, PMC develops a collaborative process between radio and television broadcasters, government ministries, and nongovernmental organizations.

The process begins by identifying cultural issues and attitudes, then analyzing the best opportunities for using mass media, and creating a comprehensive plan that includes as much of the broadcast media as possible.

Serial dramas (soap operas) have been found to be the most effective format for changing attitudes and behaviors. PMC creates serial dramas that are customized for the needs of specific regions. These dramas run over many months, and the characters gradually learn the consequences of their decisions about such things as exposure to the AIDS virus, improving the education and well-being of wives and daughters, and the benefits of smaller families.

The Whole Society Strategy combines print, television, radio, music, and Internet with training for clinic workers, journalists, and television reporters to change an entire country's ethos on reproductive health, family size, and gender equality. There is considerable hard evidence to support this approach, and the goal of PMC is no less than to bring about a more sustainable world.

Population Media Center (PMC), continued

PMC uses funding approximately as follows:
program expenses, 83%, administrative expenses,
12%, fundraising expenses, 5%.
For further information:
Website: www.populationmedia.org
Address: P.O. Box 547, Shelburne, Vermont,
    USA 05482
Telephone: 802-985-8156
Email: info@populationmedia.org

Pick One
How to Protect Animal Rights
and Wildlife Worldwide

World Wildlife Fund (WWF)

The purpose of WWF is to preserve the diversity and abundance of life on earth and the health of ecological systems. Founded in 1961, it has become the world's largest multinational conservation organization with 1.2 million members in the U.S. and 5 million worldwide

WWF helps to safeguard hundreds of species around the world and gives special attention to giant pandas, tigers, snow leopards, grizzly bears, rhinos, elephants, great apes, marine turtles, and whales and dolphins. The organization is known for its sound science and uses leading scientists to re-establish breeding programs for endangered species and protect the delicate diversity of ecosystems. WWF's habitat protection focuses on 19 areas of the world that are at most risk; these include rainforests, deserts, large freshwater systems, coral reefs, and fishing grounds.

Traffic International, a part of WWF, monitors worldwide trade in animals and animal products while fighting illegal and/or unsustainable trading practices.

WWF has received many awards as an outstanding charity for effectiveness.

WWF uses funding approximately as follows: program expenses, 83%, administrative expenses, 6%, fundraising expenses, 11%.
For more information:
Website: www.worldwildlifefund.org
Address: 1250 24th St. NVV, Washington, DC 20090
Donations to: PO Box 97180, Washington, DC 20090
Telephone: 800-960-0993
Email: membership@wwfus.org

PICK ONE
HOW TO PROTECT ANIMAL RIGHTS
AND WILDLIFE WORLDWIDE

International Fund for Animal Welfare (IFAW)

In 1969 a small group of courageous animal welfare activists brought international attention to the slaughter of Canadian seal pups (now it is illegal to hunt them). Now, four decades later, IFAW works to improve the welfare of wild and domestic animals throughout the world by reducing commercial exploitation of animals, protecting wildlife habitats, and assisting animals in distress. From its inception, IFAW rejected the idea that the welfare of animals is incompatible with the prosperity of humans. Instead they believe that the fate and welfare of animals is inseparable from that of people.

IFAW's staff of experienced campaigners, legal experts, and scientists is supported by more than 1.2 million contributors worldwide. This broad base makes it possible for IFAW to engage communities, government leaders, and like-minded organizations around the world and achieve lasting solutions to pressing animal welfare and conservation challenges.

The organization is active in a wide variety of operations, including anti-whaling, rescue of animals in distress (such as after oil spills), the support of sanctuaries, the fight against poaching, and illegal animal trade, to name a few.

International Fund for Animal Welfare (IFAW), continued

IFAW uses funding approximately as follows: program expenses, 76%, administrative expenses, 9%, fundraising expenses, 15%
For further information:
Website: www/ifaw.org
Address: 290 Summer St., Yarmouth Port, MA 02675
Telephone: 800-932-4329
Fax: 508-744-2009
Email: info@ifaw.org

PICK ONE
HOW TO PROTECT ANIMAL RIGHTS
AND WILDLIFE WORLDWIDE

People for the Ethical Treatment of Animals (PETA)

Founded in 1980, PETA is the largest animal rights organization in the world, with some 1.8 million members worldwide. PETA believes that animals feel pain, pleasure, fear, frustration, loneliness, and motherly love, and that whenever we consider doing something that would interfere with their needs, we are morally obligated to take these feelings into account. They insist that animals have an inherent worth—a value completely separate from their usefulness to humans. They believe that every creature with a will to live has a right to live free from pain and suffering, and that animals do not exist solely for human use.

PETA establishes and defends the rights of all animals and focuses especially on four areas in which the most animals suffer: factory farming, laboratory experimentation and testing, the fur trade, and the entertainment industry.

To this end PETA employs a broad range of activities, including cruelty investigations, animal rescue, animal rights legislation, research on alternatives to abusive animal testing, protest campaigns, spay and neuter programs, etc. It organizes grassroots educational campaigns that encourage respectful treatment of animals and promote alternatives to every abusive animal use. PETA also carries out protest campaigns to change the behavior of industry and commercial operations (for example, it succeeded in pressuring McDonald's to change the way their suppliers treat chickens).

People for the Ethical Treatment of Animals (PETA),
continued

PETA uses funding approximately as follows:
program expenses, 84%, administrative expenses, 4%,
fundraising expenses, $12%.
For further information:
Website: www.peta.org
Address: 501 Front St., Norfolk, VA 23510
Telephone: 757-622-7382
Fax: 757-628-0786
Email: donations@peta.org

Pick One
How to Protect Animal Rights and Wildlife Worldwide

Wildlife Conservation Society (WCS)

Founded in 1895, WCS has worked to save wildlife and wild lands throughout the world. Their goal is to change attitudes toward nature so that people and wildlife can live in sustainable interaction on both a local and a global scale.

Led by their flagship Bronx Zoo, WCS manages the world's largest system of urban wildlife parks. By combining the resources of urban wildlife parks with field projects around the world, WCS helps sustain the planet's biodiversity and provides leadership in environmental education.

To sustain biodiversity, WCS helps protect wild landscapes in North America, Latin America, Africa, and Asia—53 countries in all—and has helped save countless species from tigers to butterflies. It does this through a combination of careful science and expert management in the field.

Another important part of the organization's work is its large outreach programs that provide environmental education to literally millions of people nationally and internationally.

WCS uses funding approximately as follows: program expenses, 85%, administrative expenses, 11%, fundraising expenses, 4%.
For further information:
Website: www.wcs.org
Address: 2300 Southern Blvd., Bronx, NY 10460
Telephone: 718-220-5100
Email: development@wcs.org

PICK ONE
HOW TO PROTECT ANIMAL RIGHTS
AND WILDLIFE WORLDWIDE

Bat Conservation International (BCI)

Why bats in particular? Most bats are valuable and necessary allies of humans. They save farmers and foresters billions of dollars annually by consuming vast numbers of insect pests. And by keeping insect populations in balance, bats prevent the spread of human diseases. Yet in the Western Hemisphere and in many parts of the world they are among the most endangered land mammals. This is due to development and to misunderstandings that cause persecution. For example, it is mistakenly believed that bats pose a significant threat from rabies when humans are bitten. But in fact this is extremely rare, and humans are much more likely to get rabies from a dog or from another wild animal than from a bat.

BCI was founded in 1982 as scientists became concerned that ecosystem balance was in danger due to the alarming decline of bat populations. Since that time BCI has sought and achieved protection for the most important bat caves and has saved millions of bats through changes in the way mines are closed. Without its timely intervention, there would be far fewer bats in the world today.

The organization now has more than 14,000 members in 70 countries. It has trained hundreds of wildlife managers in 12 countries in bat management, and it supports training for graduate students in 33 countries.

Bats are an invaluable and irreplaceable resource, and BCI has demonstrated that humans and bats are not in conflict but can live together with great mutual benefit. Because bats are still misunderstood in many parts of the world they remain among the most endangered wildlife. BCI continues to make an extremely important contribution to the maintenance of healthy ecosystems.

Bat Conservation International (BCI), continued

BCI uses funding approximately as follows:
program expenses, 80%, administrative expenses, 8%,
fundraising expenses, 12%.
For further information:
Website: www.batcon.org
HQ address: 500 N Capital of Texas Hwy, Bldg. 1,
    Suite 200, Austin, TX 78746
Mail donations to: PO Box 162603, Austin, TX 78716
Telephone: 512-327-9721
Fax: 512-327-9724
Email: development@batcon.org

PICK ONE
HOW TO HELP ENDANGERED
TRIBES SURVIVE

Cultural Survival (CS)

CS is an organization dedicated to the idea that indigenous people should be able to live safely on their own lands and on their own terms. Starting in the 1960s, CS has worked with indigenous communities in Africa, Asia, Australia, and North and South America, and has become the leading U.S.-based organization defending the rights of indigenous people everywhere.

The organization works in partnership with indigenous people to defend their rights of self-determination which includes the rights to their lands, resources, languages, and cultures. All CS projects are designed to be self-sustaining, *and the projects are run entirely by indigenous people*. When their governments don't protect their rights, CS brings their cases to international commissions and courts.

Staffed with respected indigenous leaders, anthropologists, human rights lawyers, and entrepreneurs, a significant part of CS's effort is its international, public outreach program. For more than 30 years, CS has been the most comprehensive and trusted source of information on indigenous issues of any organization in the world.

The Cultural Survival Quarterly is the respected CS publication that covers global indigenous subjects. Cultural Survival Voices, its newsletter, is sent to more than 350 indigenous organizations around the world, providing them with the practical information they need to defend their rights. All of the information contained in these publications is available on the CS website.

Cultural Survival (CS), continued

CS uses funding approximately as follows:
program expenses, 84%, administrative expenses, 7%,
fundraising expenses, 9%.
For further information:
Website: www.culturalsurvival.org
Address: 215 Prospect Street, Cambridge, MA 02139
Telephone: 617-441-5400
Fax: 617-441-5417
Email: culturalsurvival@cs.org

PICK ONE
HOW TO HELP ENDANGERED
TRIBES SURVIVE

Survival International (SI)

SI was founded in 1969 to help the approximately 200 million tribal people in the world to survive and to ensure that the interests of tribal people are properly presented in all decisions affecting their future.

Headquartered in London, SI has some 12,000 members in 75 countries. Working to help tribal people in 30 countries, some of SI's successes include: recognition and restoration of Yanomami land rights in Brazil; return of Martu Aborigines to their native tribal lands in Western Australia; and saving the lands of 20,000 Aka Pygmies who are hunter-gatherers in the Central African Republic.

SI has an extensive outreach program on behalf of endangered tribes that includes teaching materials for schools and the issuance of urgent action bulletins to take action against specific threats.

The organization has received the Right Livelihood Award from the Swedish government, widely know as the "Alternate Nobel Prize" for social transformation.

SI has also received national awards from the governments of Spain and Italy for its work.

SI uses funding approximately as follows:
program expenses, 91%, administrative expenses, 1%, fundraising expenses, 9%.
For further information:
Website: www.survival-international.org
Address: 6 Charterhouse Bldg., London
   EC1M 7ET, UK
Telephone: 44 (0)20 7687 8700
Email: info@survival-international.org

PICK ONE
HOW TO HELP ENDANGERED
TRIBES SURVIVE

Amazon Alliance (AA)

Founded in 1990, AA is a collaboration of more than 100 member organizations whose aim is to eliminate cultural and environmental degradation in Amazonia. Members consist of local indigenous groups and environmental organizations who work together as equals. AA ensures that the region's indigenous people have a voice and actual power to determine the processes that affect their communities. This organization is the only one that is able to coordinate the many diverse stakeholders of the region.

AA identifies problem areas and then coordinates with member groups to provide:

- Communication between members
- Support for members that can influence actions
- An exchange of skills between members
- Information about potential donors
- Contacts with international media

Development in Amazonia is rapidly moving forward under the auspices of the Initiative for the Integration of Regional Infrastructure in South America (IIRSA). But indigenous leaders and groups have not been included in the planning and implementation of this large-scale endeavor. AA is working to include legitimate indigenous voices in the initiative and to provide them with more direct access to international funding so that their voices are heard.

AA is providing timely information about climate change to indigenous groups. It is also providing expert legal support in developing a team of skilled, indigenous negotiators. It is the aim of AA to have these local negotiators able to engage with the designers and implementers of IIRSA to create more balanced and fair development outcomes.

With the goal of creating a cohesive action plan for the whole of Amazonia, AA is launching forums which will bring together hundreds of indigenous and non-profit leaders.

AA uses funding approximately as follows:
program expenses, 90%, administrative expenses, 6%,
fundraising expenses, 4%.
For further information:
Website: www.amazonalliance.org
Address: 1350 Connecticut Ave. NW, Ste. 1100,
    Washington, D.C. 20036
Telephone: 202-785-3334
Email: amazon@amazonalliance.org

National, Regional, and Community Charities

PICK ONE
DISASTER RELIEF — THE NATION

American Red Cross (ARC)

This venerable organization has rendered assistance in emergencies for 126 years, providing food, lodging, health services, crisis interventions, and community mental-health services as well as other related emergency care to persons in need. Through more than 750 locally supported chapters, more than 15 million people each year take ARC training courses to prepare for and respond to emergencies in their own homes and in their communities. Almost four million people give blood through the Red Cross, making it the largest supplier of blood and blood products in the U.S.

Through its Armed Forces Emergency Services program the Red Cross provides military members, veterans, and their families with emergency communications, help in obtaining financial assistance for expenses related to emergency travel or personal crisis and other vital services at U.S. military installations worldwide.

Other services include meal delivery to homebound residents, food pantries, rides to medical appointments, homeless shelters, transitional housing, caregiver education and support groups, hospital and nursing home volunteers, emergency fuel assistance, to name a few.

There has been some controversy over the ARC's speed in responding to large-scale disasters, but this organization offers so many services in so many areas of need that its very considerable benefits are indispensable to the country.

> ARC uses funding as follows: program expenses, 95%, administrative expenses, 3%, fundraising expenses, 2%.
> For further information:
> Website: www.redcross.org
> Address: 2025 E Street, Washington DC 20006
> Telephone: 202-303-4498

PICK ONE
DISASTER RELIEF — THE NATION

The Salvation Army (TSA) (a sectarian organization)

In addition to its many other services, TSA is one of the nation's largest disaster relief organizations. It holds a unique position in that its services are provided in partnership with several government agencies (including FEMA, the Federal Emergency Management Agency). TSA, though a faith-based organization, does not deny service because of a recipient's beliefs.

TSA is not a first responder; instead, it supports first responders (such as firefighters, police, emergency medics). Relief services depend on a given situation and the magnitude of the disaster. Emergency response services are activated through pre-planned, coordinated procedures with government agencies and non-government groups. Typical activities include:

- Food service. Food is delivered and prepared at a number of on-site feeding facilities, including Army mobile canteens. Food is also provided for search and rescue operations, law enforcement activities, civilian training exercises, etc.
- Hydration Service. Special beverages that replenish mineral electrolytes and other vital ingredients are stocked and dispensed.
- Emergency Shelter. TSA sets up temporary shelters in schools and other buildings designated by authorities.
- Cleanup and Restoration. TSA provides cleanup and sanitation supplies after a disaster and, as needed, distributes reconstruction supplies such as lumber and sheetrock from warehouses.
- Financial Assistance. Direct financial assistance to victims of disaster is dispensed through trained caseworkers. This assistance may be for food, clothing, medicine, bedding, medical or funeral needs.

- Emergency Communications. Through its own network and with other amateur radio groups, TSA coordinates emergency communications when other systems, such as telephones, are not working.
- Administration. This service is designed to keep all other services functioning and includes activities such as purchasing, legal documentation, reporting to appropriate government agencies and coordination of spontaneous volunteers.

TSA uses funding approximately as follows (consolidated figures from 9,347 operations centers): program expenses, 83%, administrative expenses, 12%, fundraising expenses, 5%.
For further information:
Website: www.salvationarmy.org
For general inquiries:
Address: P.O. Box 269, Alexandria, VA 22313
For donations or program inquiries, use the website
    to find contact information for local chapters.

PICK ONE
SHELTER FOR FAMILIES
IN NEED — THE NATION

National Alliance to End Homelessness (NAEH)

NAEH is an organization committed to preventing and ending homelessness in the United States. It provides research and data to policymakers and elected officials in order to inform policy debates and to enact much-need legislation. The organization has been a leader in lobbying for new, comprehensive approaches to homelessness.

NAEH has generated a national plan not just to manage homelessness but to end it.

Several decades ago, homelessness in the U.S. was not a major problem. Now, on any given night, nearly a million people will be homeless despite the expenditure of billions of dollars each year.

To end homelessness, the system needs to change. Our current system doesn't prevent people from becoming homeless, it doesn't add to the availability of housing, and it doesn't provide services that would actually end homelessness.

NAEH's national plan focuses on two basic elements. First, those who become homeless are almost always clients of mainstream agencies (welfare, health care, mental health care, substance abuse treatment, child protection, veterans' assistance, and the criminal justice system). The irony is that the more effective our homelessness assistance system is, the less incentive the other agencies have to deal with their clients' problems, which creates more homelessness. The incentives of mainstream agencies must be reversed so that homelessness can be prevented in the first place, which means changes must take place by larger efforts to help very poor people.

The second element of the NAEH national plan is to help people to exit homelessness as soon as possible. This means providing permanent supportive housing (housing with services), which saves money by reducing the use of other agencies' services.

People shouldn't spend years in homeless systems, either in shelters or in transitional housing.

Changing the homeless assistance system means including housing stability as an integral part of how agencies and nonprofit organizations assist poor people. NAEH believes that if these changes are implemented, complete institutionalization of homelessness can be avoided and homelessness can essentially be eliminated within ten years.

NAEH uses funding approximately as follows: program expenses, 92%, administrative expenses, 6%, fundraising expenses, 2%.
For further information:
Website: www.endhomelessness.org
Address: 1518 K Street NW, Ste. 410, Washington, DC 20005
Telephone: 202-638-1526
Fax: 202-638-4664
Email: naeh@naeh.org

Pick One
Shelter for Families
In Need — The Nation

Habitat for Humanity International (HFHI)

(a sectarian organization)

Founded in 1976, HFHI is a nonprofit organization whose goal is decent shelter for everyone, worldwide. The organization utilizes volunteers plus donations of money and materials to build or rehabilitate houses with the help of partner families. The houses are sold to partner families at no profit, and the monthly mortgage payments are used to build more Habitat houses. Houses are based upon need regardless of background, race, or religion.

Habitat houses are not given free. An affordable down payment and mortgage payments are required. The houses are sold to partner families at no profit and the families invest hundreds of hours building their own houses, and also help to build other Habitat houses. The cost of Habitat houses ranges from $800 in some developing countries to an average $60,000 in the U.S.

Selection of families is based on three criteria: level of need, willingness and ability to contribute sweat equity, and ability to repay the loan.

HFHI works through independent, locally run affiliates that direct all aspects of home building, including fundraising, family selection, site selection, construction, and the servicing of mortgages. Local affiliates are asked to give 10% of their received donations for house building in other countries.

HFHI has built more than 300,000 houses in countries around the world, providing decent shelter for some 1.5 million people.

Habitat for Humanity International (HFHI), continued

HFHI uses funding approximately as follows:
program expenses, 81%, administrative expenses, 4%,
fundraising expenses, 15%.
For further information:
Website: www.habitat.org
Address: 121 Habitat Street, Americus, GA 31709
Telephone: 800-422-4828
Email: publicinfo@habitat.org

PICK ONE
SHELTER FOR FAMILIES
IN NEED — THE NATION

Volunteers of America (VOA) (a sectarian organization)

VOA is one the nation's largest and most comprehensive human services organizations. Through thousands of programs, it provides services to more than two million people each year, including at-risk youth, the frail elderly, released prisoners, homeless individuals and families, the disabled, and those recovering from addictions.

VOA is one of the nation's largest providers of affordable housing for low- and moderate-income families.

VOA also provides a number of community services including holiday meals, the operation of thrift stores, and emergency services. The organization currently has some 150,000 volunteers and 15,000 employees.

VOA offers so many diverse services it would take pages to list them all. Through its disadvantaged youth program, VOA provides a continuum of care that includes prevention, early intervention, and long-term services. Special programs care for the needs of runaway and homeless children, and there are mentoring programs for the children of prisoners.

VOA has a long history of serving persons who are re-entering society after periods of incarceration. The organization partners with local communities to offer acceptance, guidance, and appropriate employment to the formerly incarcerated.

The organization is a major provider of long-term nursing care for seniors and others coping with illness or injury, and it has programs for substance abuse, employment training, transportation for health care, etc.

See the section in this book on volunteering for a description of the organization's extensive volunteer activities.

Volunteers of America (VOA), continued

VOA uses funding approximately as follows:
program expenses, 89%, administrative expenses,
8.5%, fundraising expenses, 2.5%.
For further information:
Website: www.voa.org
Address: 1660 Duke Street, Alexandria, VA 22314
Telephone: 800-899-0089
Fax: 703-341-7000
Email: kmcbride@voa.org

PICK ONE
SHELTER FOR FAMILIES
IN NEED — THE NATION

Enterprise Community Partners (ECP)

ECP, a nonprofit organization, is a leading provider of the financing and expertise required to create affordable housing units in the U.S. Recipients of housing are working-class families, elderly people, and those displaced by poverty or natural disaster

The organization creates affordable housing by partnering with government agencies, banks, and community groups. To date it has raised $8 billion to help build or preserve some 225,000 decent, affordable homes, and is currently investing in communities at the rate of $1 billion per year.

ECP leverages private financing with public funding programs (such as grants from the U.S. Department of Housing and Urban Development [HUD] and the Federal Home Loan Banks) to acquire land and arrange for site preparation and housing construction.

ECP has formed a partnership with another nonprofit, the Corporation for Supportive Housing, to create the Supportive Housing Investment Partnership (SHIP). This partnership offers grants, loans, and tax credits to help developers create thousands of affordable housing units, including medical care, substance abuse counseling, and other needed services for homeless persons or those at risk of becoming homeless.

The goal of this partnership is no less than to end homelessness in America.

Enterprise Community Partners (ECP), continued

ECP uses funding approximately as follows:
program expenses, 79.5%, administrative
expenses, 18.5%, fundraising expenses, 2%.
For further information:
Website: www.enterprisefoundation.org
Address: 10227 Wincopin Circle, American City
    Bldg., Columbia, MD 21044
Telephone: 800- 624-4298
Fax: 410-964-1918
Email: swilliams@enterprisecommunity.org

PICK ONE
HOW TO HELP PROVIDE
HEALTH CARE TO PEOPLE
IN NEED — THE NATION

United Way (UW)

United Way is a national network of nearly 1,300 local organizations that work to advance the common good by focusing on education, income, and health. United Way of America is the national organization that coordinates and assists the local chapters. Local chapters focus on childhood obesity, health insurance coverage, healthcare quality, childhood immunizations, substance abuse, family violence, oral health, and other healthcare concerns voiced by the local community.

As well as supporting local health programs, UW partners with local advocates, faith leaders, healthcare professionals, the business community, and local government to assist and coordinate comprehensive health services. In communities across the U.S., United Way contributions and the many volunteers in local chapters play a significant role in improving access to quality health care.

While most contributions to UW are made through payroll deduction plans, donors can make individual contributions and can specify how their donations are used. Only 1% of donations go to help maintain the national organization—the rest is directed by volunteers to local needs.

United Way (UW), continued

The national UW organization uses its funding approx-
imately as follows: program expenses, 89%, admin-
istrative expenses, 10%, fundraising expenses, 1%.
For further information:
To locate your local United Way, enter your zip
    code on the national website.
National website: www.liveunited.org
Address: 701 N. Fairfax St., Alexandria, VA 22314
Telephone: 703-836-7100
Email: plannedgiving@unitedway.org

PICK ONE
HOW TO HELP PROVIDE
HEALTH CARE TO PEOPLE
IN NEED — THE NATION

Remote Area Medical Foundation (RAMF)

RAMF is the nonprofit foundation that funds the RAM Volunteer Corps (RAMVC). RAMVC is a nonprofit, all-volunteer, airborne relief corps dedicated to serving mankind by providing free health care, dental care, eye care, and veterinary services to people in remote areas of the United States and the world.

Founded in 1985, RAM began by airlifting medical personnel to very remote areas of the world, but the leaders discovered that there are also vast numbers of people in the U.S. who are in desperate need of medical care. Now, American volunteer doctors, nurses, pilots, veterinarians, and support workers participate in programs *at their own expense* in areas of the country where medical care is either inaccessible or people cannot afford what care is available.

This remarkable organization airlifts medical personnel and equipment to areas deemed to be in need and sets up massive, temporary clinics, typically for one weekend. Over the course of a weekend, hundreds to a few thousand individuals are treated on the spot, without any charge. These weekend clinics often have lines of hundreds of uninsured or underinsured people, waiting their turn for the chance of high quality, free treatment. No qualifications are required—everyone who shows up is treated (except when the lines are so long that some must be turned away).

So far, some 26,000 doctors, dentists, nurses, and medical support people have left the comfort of their homes and families to treat more than 300,000 patients. With RAM, all medical supplies, medicines, facilities, and vehicles are donated; and the entire operation functions on a tiny, shoestring budget that is almost unbelievable considering what is accomplished.

Remote Area Medical Foundation (RAMF), continued

RAMF uses funding approximately as follows:
program expenses, 87%, administrative
expenses, 11%, fundraising expenses, 2%.
For further information:
Website: www.ramusa.org
Address: 1834 Beech St., Knoxville, TN 37920
Telephone: 865-579-1530
Fax: 865-609-1876

Pick One
How to Help Provide
Health Care to People
in Need — the Nation

Shriners Hospitals for Children

Shriners Hospitals for Children is a one-of-a-kind international health-care system of 22 hospitals dedicated to improving the lives of children by providing specialty pediatric care as well as innovative research and teaching programs. Children from birth up to age 18 with orthopedic conditions, burns, spinal cord injuries, and cleft lip and palate are eligible for care and receive all services at no charge. Acceptance is based solely on a child's medical needs. A family's income, insurance status, or lack of affiliation with a Shriner have no bearing on a child's acceptance as a patient.

Since 1922, Shriners Hospitals have treated more than 835,000 children from around the world without charge. The hospitals, at their 22 separate locations, employ over 6,000 employees, most of whom are highly trained health care professionals.

The organization accepts no funds from government agencies or insurance companies and relies on donations from the public and the efforts of the Shrine of North America.

Shriners uses funding as follows: program expenses, 93%, administrative expenses, 6%, fundraising expenses, 1%.
For further information:
Website: shrinershq.org
Address: 2900 Rocky Point Drive, Tampa, FL 33607
Telephone: 813-281-0300
Email: emcgonigal@shrinenet.org

PICK ONE
HOW TO HELP ALLEVIATE
HUNGER — THE NATION

Feeding America (FA)

Feeding America, formerly called America's Second Harvest, is the nation's largest charitable hunger relief organization. FA serves all 50 states plus the District of Columbia and Puerto Rico and supports some 50,000 local charitable agencies, including food pantries, soup kitchens, emergency shelters, after-school programs, and Kids Cafes. Each year, in the U.S., the organization provides food assistance to more than 25 million low income, hungry people.

FA operates nationally to obtain food from corporate donors and distributes it, as needed, to local food banks. Also, due to its close working relationship with the federal government, FA is the primary recipient of government commodities, such as those from the Emergency Food Assistance Program.

Working as a national organization, FA is able to coordinate the requirements of local food banks so that food products are distributed to where they are needed. This avoids the situation where one local food bank receives an excess of a certain commodity while another is short of that product.

FA also provides training for local food banks in the efficient distribution of food and sets standards for food safety, transportation, donor relations, and transparency and accountability.

Every dollar donated to FA helps provide 20 pounds of food and grocery products to men, women, and children facing hunger in the U.S.

FA is one of the most efficient of major charities and receives the highest rating from charity rating organizations.

Feeding America (FA), continued

FA uses funding approximately as follows:
program expenses, 98%, administrative expenses, 1%,
fundraising expenses, 1%.
For further information:
Website: www.feedingamerica.org
Address: 35 East Wacker Dr., Ste. 2000, Chicago,
    IL 60601
Telephone: 800-771-2303
Email: fundraise@feedingamerica.org

PICK ONE
HOW TO HELP ALLEVIATE
HUNGER — THE NATION

Meals on Wheels Association of America (MOWAA)

MOWAA and MOWAAF, their supporting foundation, are the national organizations that support all the local Meals on Wheels programs across the U.S. Local Meals on Wheels (MOW) programs deliver hot, ready-to-eat meals to homebound persons who cannot provide their own meals. Recipients include the elderly, sick and disabled persons, and bedridden women with high-risk pregnancies. Some recipients require long-term help while others are only temporary.

Services to elderly, frail individuals often allow them to remain in their homes and avoid being placed in institutions. In addition to delivering meals, this service provides a safety check on the health or other needs of a recipient.

Some local programs suggest voluntary contributions from recipients if they are able, while others charge modest fees. However, eligibility to receive meals is determined solely be medical need, and no one is turned away if there is an inability to pay.

The national association, MOWAA, provides funding, technical support, and training for local programs.

Limited resources and a growing need are straining the capacity of MOW programs. In particular, programs in rural areas are hard hit because of the times and distances required to make deliveries. MOWAA is developing a national plan, involving corporate, nonprofit, and academic input, to address this problem.

MOWAA has also developed guidelines and training programs for emergency preparedness to enable local MOW workers to respond to events that can disrupt deliveries.

The goal of the national association's foundation, in addition to supporting the work of MOWAA, is to become the nation's primary authority and information source for senior nutrition and hunger programs.

Meals on Wheels Association of America (MOWAA), continued

MOWAA uses funding approximately as follows: program expenses, 85%, administrative expenses, 10%, fundraising expenses, 5%.
For further information:
Website: www.mowaa.org
Address: 203 S. Union St., Alexandria, VA 22314
Telephone: 703-548-5558
Email: mowaa@mowaa.org

PICK ONE
HOW TO HELP PROMOTE NUTRITION AND FOOD SAFETY — THE NATION

Center for Science in the Public Interest (CSPI)

As one of the nation's top consumer advocates since 1971, CSPI has fought for government policies and corporate practices that promote healthy diets, prevent deceptive marketing practices, and ensure that science is used to promote the public welfare. Its award-winning newsletter, *Nutrition Action Healthletter*, with some 900,000 subscribers in the United States and Canada, is the largest-circulation health newsletter in North America; and the organization itself, has won awards for its service from the U.S. Food and Drug Administration (FDA).

CSPI's accomplishments include leading the efforts to win passage of laws that require nutrition facts on packaged foods, define the term "organic" for foods, and put warning notices on alcoholic beverages. CSPI has also conducted studies on the nutritional quality of restaurant meals, helped to increase funding for the government's food safety inspections, and promoted healthy nutrition and physical activity programs for schools. Among its several areas of interest, CSPI is currently working to get junk foods out of schools, eliminate the use of harmful trans fats and reduce sodium in processed foods, reduce the incidence of food borne illnesses by improving food safety laws, and expose industry influence over the scientific studies of nutrition.

Center for Science in the Public Interest (CSPI),
continued

CSPI uses funding approximately as follows:
program expenses, 86%, administrative expenses,
2.5%, fundraising expenses, 11.5%.
For further information:
Website: www.cspinet.org
Address: 1875 Connecticut Avenue NW, Ste. 300,
    Washington, DC 20009
Telephone: 202-332-9110
Fax: 202-265-4954
Email cspi@cspinet.org

Pick One
How to Help Promote Nutrition and Food Safety — The Nation

Center for Food Safety (CFS)

CFS was founded in 1997 for the purpose of protecting human health and the environment by curbing the proliferation of harmful food production technologies and by promoting organic and other forms of safe and sustainable agriculture. It does this by acting as a watchdog for the policies of the nation's primary agencies involved in regulating food supply, which are: the Food and Drug Administration (FDA), the U.S. Department of Agriculture (USDA), and the Environmental Protection Agency (EPA).

The organization influences legislation, creates litigation when harmful practices are discovered, promotes public education, and provides technical assistance to numerous other nonprofit organizations involved in food safety.

CFS staff work to educate consumers and develop public support for all the organization's actions. CFS supports an extensive grassroots action network, the True Food Network, which is a good source to learn more about all issues surrounding agricultural production and the foods we eat.

CFS is active in a number of areas, including monitoring the safety of genetically modified foods, livestock cloning, fish farms, hormones and food irradiation, use of antibiotics, using sewage sludge as fertilizer, pesticide and herbicide use, health labeling, and criteria for "organic" labeling.

Center for Food Safety (CFS), continued

CFS uses funding as follows: program expenses, 86.5%, administrative expenses, 6%, fundraising expenses, 7.5%.

For further information:

Website: www.centerforfoodsafety.org

Address: 660 Pennsylvania Avenue, SE, Suite 302,
  Washington, DC 20003

Telephone: 800-600-6664

Fax: 202-547-9429

Email: office@centerforfoodsafety.org

PICK ONE
HOW TO HELP PROMOTE NUTRITION
AND FOOD SAFETY — THE NATION

Public Citizen (PC)

Public Citizen was founded in 1971 as a national, nonprofit advocacy (lobbying) organization to represent citizens' interests in Congress and the executive and judicial branches of government. It has a history of fierce independence and considerable success in the fight for openness and accountability in government. PC has upheld the rights of consumers for a great many issues, including social and economic justice, individual safety, environmental protection, effective and affordable health care, fair trade policies, campaign finance reform, transparent governance, etc.

Among its long string of achievements: In 1974 PC successfully lobbied Congress to override a presidential veto to make strong improvements to the Freedom of Information Act. In 1976 PC stopped the use of a toxic red dye in foods and the use of chloroform in cough medicines and toothpaste. In 1981 PC thwarted President Reagan's attempt to abolish the Clean Air Act. In 1983 PC stopped the administration's attempt to revoke auto safety standards (air bags). In 1987 PC won a landmark court order prohibiting banks from holding checks for excessive time periods. In 1989 PC forced Congress to halt its exorbitant, self-determined pay raise and to prohibit financial awards (honoraria) to legislators. In 1990 PC forced the Nuclear Regulatory Commission to require minimum training standards for nuclear reactor workers. In 1992 PC won a court order forcing the Occupational Safety and Hazard Commission (OSHA) to halt the exposure of workers to toxic cadmium. In 1994 PC played a key role in making home equity scams illegal. In 1998 PC forced publication of a national list of doctors disciplined for malpractice and other malfeasance. In 1999 PC played a key role in passing truck safety legislation which resulted in the creation of the Motor Carrier Safety Administration, and it led the coalition that forced Firestone to recall 6.5 million defective auto tires. And so on.

PC is a lobbying organization and donations to it are not tax deductible. Donations to PCF, the Public Citizen Foundation, are for education and are tax deductible.

Because PC requires a large staff for its work, its administrative costs are higher than for similar charities. PC uses funding approximately as follows: program expenses, 65%, administrative expenses, 24%, fundraising expenses, 11%. PCF uses funding approximately as follows: program expenses, 85.5 %, administrative expenses, 9.5%, fundraising expenses, 5%.

For further information on both organizations:

Website: www.citizen.org

Address: 1600 20th Street, NW, Washington, DC 20009

Telephone: 202-588-1000

Email: member@citizen.org

Pick One
How to Help Eliminate
Poverty — The Nation

While a number of nonprofit organizations that do charitable work in the U.S. fight poverty by doing peripheral work (such as in homelessness, substance abuse, care for the disabled, operating thrift stores, education and jobs for at-risk youth, etc.), it is our belief that the United Way is one of the few that focus directly on reducing poverty, and because of this it is our sole listing.

United Way

United Way is a national network of nearly 1,300 local organizations that work to advance the common good by focusing on education, income, and health.

Recent statistics show that almost one-third of American families do not earn enough income to meet their basic needs. In addition to the continuing work of local chapters and volunteers to help raise income levels, United Way has created the Financial Stability Network™ which will commit $1.5 billion to identify and improve the underlying causes of the financial hardship facing today's families. United Way will coordinate cross-sector partnerships to empower them with the tools and skills necessary to maximize their income, build savings, and gain assets. This will entail the active participation of Fortune 500 businesses, nonprofit organizations, federal agencies, and all local United Way chapters.

Among other elements, this program will include:

- Increase the number of families eligible for the earned income tax credit (EITC) but who are not claiming it.
- Reduce the number of families who do not have access to credit, low-interest loans, and banking services in general.
- Through the use of the latest technology, enable all United Way chapters to enroll eligible families in earned public benefits that have not been claimed.

- Provide financial education to low-income families on how to develop and sustain savings programs, how to maximize assets and how to enter the financial mainstream, along with credit repair and debt services.
- Provide free tax assistance and tax form preparation.
- Provide workforce training and any needed remedial education for job placement skills.
- Provide needed transportation, child care, and other support services.
- Through corporate and local partnerships, offer matching incentives to help families accumulate savings for lantern assets such as a house, higher education for children, small businesses, etc.

Although United Way has for many years been a major player in the effort to improve the lives of low-income individuals and families, a program of this nature has never been tried before on such a huge scale and with so many participating partners. Its success depends in part on individual donations and volunteer efforts.

While most contributions to United Way are made through payroll deduction plans, donors can make individual contributions and can specify how their donations are used. Only 1% of donations go to help maintain the national organization—the rest is directed by volunteers to local needs.

The national organization uses its funding approximately as follows: program expenses, 89%, administrative expenses, 10%, fundraising expenses, 1%.
For further information:
To locate your local United Way, enter your zip code on the national website.
National website: www.liveunited.org
Address: 701 N. Fairfax St., Alexandria, VA 22314
Telephone: 703-836-7100
Email: plannedgiving@unitedway.org

PICK ONE
HOW TO HELP CHILDREN
THE NATION

Save the Children Federation (SC)

SC, founded in 1932, is one of the leading organizations that provide comprehensive help to children in the U.S. and throughout the world. Their programs focus on a wide range of assistance, including health, hunger, literacy, protection from violence, and disaster relief. SC serves millions of children and the adults who care for them. Those involved include parents, community members, local organizations, and government agencies.

Education programs emphasize basic learning, both formal and informal, that help children and adults develop reading, writing, and mathematics skills. SC's health programs focus on the survival, health, and development of women and children, emphasizing child survival, reproductive health (including family planning, safe motherhood, and HIV/STD prevention), and nutrition.

In the United States, SC serves children in rural communities in 13 states. It is also providing assistance to Gulf Coast children forced from their homes as a result of Hurricanes Katrina and Rita. SC trains members of community organizations, tribal groups, and schools in some of the United States' poorest places to provide literacy, physical activity, and nutrition programming during out-of-school hours.

Individual child and community sponsorships are available. Local field offices monitor and report on local services and progress to ensure that sponsored children are benefiting from these programs. Child sponsors annually receive updated information on their sponsored child, the current programs, projects in the child's community, and the challenges faced by those living in the community.

Save the Children Federation (SC), continued

SC uses funding approximately as follows:
program expenses, 90%, administrative expenses, 4%,
fundraising expenses, 6%.
For further information:
Website: www.savethechildren.org
Address: 54 Wilton Road, Westport, CT 06880
Telephone: 800-728-3843
Email: twebster@savechildren.org

PICK ONE
HOW TO HELP CHILDREN
THE NATION

Make-A-Wish Foundation of America

Beginning in 1980 by granting the wish of a single child with a life-threatening medical condition, Make-A-Wish has grown to include some 25,000 volunteers who have reached more than 150,000 children. Volunteers serve as wish granters, fundraisers, special events assistants, and in several other capacities. On average, a child's wish is granted every 41 minutes.

Make-A-Wish grants the wishes of children with life-threatening medical conditions from age 2½ to 18.

A parent, doctor, or even the child can initiate a wish request. Make-A-Wish sends a special wish team to meet with the child, explore suggestions, and learn his or her one true wish. Wishes have included such things as going to theme parks, meeting favorite celebrities, getting computers, having special parties, getting pets, and shopping sprees.

There are 69 local Make-A-Wish chapters in the U.S. and the U.S. territories of Guam and Puerto Rico. Individual donors, corporations, and diverse organizations support the foundation.

Make-A-Wish uses funding as follows:
program expenses, 75%, administrative expenses, 10%, fundraising expenses, 15%.
For further information:
Website: www.wish.org
Address: PO Box 29119, Phoenix, AZ 85038
Telephone: 866-880-1382
Email: mawfa@wish.org

Pick One
How to Help Children
The Nation

Shriners Hospitals for Children

Shriners Hospitals for Children is a one-of-a-kind international health care system of 22 hospitals dedicated to improving the lives of children by providing specialty pediatric care as well as innovative research and teaching programs. Children from birth up to age 18 with orthopedic conditions, burns, spinal cord injuries, and cleft lip and palate are eligible for care and receive all services at no charge. Acceptance is based solely on a child's medical needs. A family's income, insurance status, or lack of affiliation with a Shriner have no bearing on a child's acceptance as a patient.

Since 1922, Shriners Hospitals have treated more than 835,000 children from around the world without charge. The hospitals, at their 22 separate locations, employ over 6,000 employees, most of whom are highly trained health care professionals.

The organization accepts no funds from government agencies or insurance companies and relies on donations from the public and the efforts of the Shrine of North America.

Shriners uses funding as follows: program expenses, 93%, administrative expenses, 6%, fundraising expenses, 1%.
For further information:
Website: shrinershq.org
Address: 2900 Rocky Point Dr., Tampa, FL 33607
Telephone: 813-281-0300
Email: emcgonigal@shrinenet.org

PICK ONE
HOW TO HELP CHILDREN
THE NATION

Kids Against Hunger (KAH)

Founded in 1999, KAH packages and distributes specially developed, nutritionally complete food packages to hungry children in the U.S. and to starving children in developing countries.

The organization purchases raw ingredients that are specially formulated by food scientists to provide easily digested protein, carbohydrates, and vitamins necessary to prevent malnutrition and hunger-related diseases in children. The food packages are simple to prepare in that they require only boiling water to make a complete meal.

Since its inception, and with the help of more than 100,000 volunteers, KAH has sent some millions of food meals to children, including a million meals sent to victims of Hurricane Katrina. Shipping is provided either by the U.S. Government or by recipient humanitarian organizations.

Volunteers package ingredients at the main facility in Minnesota and at some 30 independently run satellite facilities in 19 states and one in Canada. The entire network has the capacity to produce more than 20 million meals each year.

KAH takes special care to ship food packs only to places where the recipient organization is trusted to distribute it to needy children.

KAH receives funding from individual donors, corporations, foundations, churches, and synagogues. All satellite facilities are separate nonprofit organizations.

Kids Against Hunger (KAH), continued

KAH national uses funding approximately as follows: program expenses, 71%, administrative expenses, 14%, fundraising expenses, 15%. (Note: KAH receives on-going support from an anonymous company for overhead so that some 90% of individual donations go directly toward food purchases.)
For further information:
Website: www.feedingchildren.org
Address: 5401 Boone Ave N, New Hope, MN 55428
Telephone: 866-654-0202
Fax: 763-504-2943
Email: info@kidsagainsthunger.com

PICK ONE
HOW TO HELP CHILDREN
THE NATION

Volunteers of America (VOA) (a sectarian organization)

VOA is one the nation's largest and most comprehensive human services organizations. Through thousands of programs, it provides services to more than two million people each year, including at-risk youth, the frail elderly, released prisoners, homeless individuals and families, the disabled and those recovering from addictions. VOA also provides a number of community services including holiday meals, the operation of thrift stores, and emergency services. The organization currently has some 95,000 volunteers and 15,000 employees.

VOA offers so many diverse services it would take pages to list them all. Through its disadvantaged youth program, VOA provides a continuum of care that includes prevention, early intervention, and long-term services. Special programs care for the needs of runaway and homeless children, and there are mentoring programs for the children of prisoners.

VOA has a long history of serving persons who are re-entering society after periods of incarceration. The organization partners with local communities to offer acceptance, guidance, and appropriate employment to the formerly incarcerated.

The organization is a major provider of long-term nursing care for seniors and others coping with illness or injury, and it has programs for substance abuse, employment training, transportation for health care, etc. VOA is also one of the nation's largest providers of affordable housing for low- and moderate-income families.

See the organization's website for listings of needed volunteers in your area.

Volunteers of America (VOA), continued

VOA uses funding approximately as follows:
program expenses, 89%, administrative expenses,
8.5%, fundraising expenses, 2.5%.
For further information:
Website: www.voa.org
Address: 1660 Duke Street, Alexandria, VA 22314
Telephone: 800-899-0089
Fax: 703-341-7000
Email: kmcbride@voa.org

PICK ONE
HOW TO HELP CHILDREN
THE NATION

Child Find of America (CFA)

CFA is an organization that works to prevent or resolve all cases of missing, abducted, or runaway children. Founded in 1980 by a mother of a missing child, today CFA helps thousands of families locate their missing children, resolve family custody disputes, and/or arrange for safe custody in a legal environment through mediation. CFA works in all 50 states (and in more than a dozen other countries).

Each year CFA receives thousands of calls for assistance from parents and other family members, law enforcement, and child protection agencies.

When CFA was founded there was a lack of understanding of the effects on a child of abduction, and little response by law enforcement. The organization played a leading role in the enactment of laws that now make all forms of child abduction a crime. It created a national clearinghouse to aid law enforcement agencies and influenced the media to publicize missing children cases.

CFA now offers a full range of services to families, including ways of preventing abductions and runaways, conflict resolution, missing child investigation, support services, and referrals to other involved agencies. CFA staff members investigate each case of a missing child, using the Internet and a very large network that includes local and state law enforcement agencies, the FBI, and schools. Photos of missing children are distributed throughout the country via the media, businesses, and volunteers. In cases of family conflict, CFA helps prevent abduction or other harm to children by maintaining a national network of experienced, volunteer mediators.

CFA has now become the national authority in the prevention and resolution of child abductions. It has received the highest ratings from major charity rating organizations and has been named by Worth Magazine as one of America's 100 best charities.

> CFA uses funding approximately as follows: program expenses, 94%, administrative expenses, 4.5%, fundraising expenses, 1.5%.
> For further information:
> Website: www.childfindofamerica.org
> Address: PO Box 277, New Paltz, NY 12561
> Telephone: 845-883-6060
> Fax: 845-691-7766
> Email: information@childfindofamerica.org

PICK ONE
HOW TO HELP PROMOTE
EDUCATION — THE NATION

Reader To Reader (RTR)

The most recent estimate indicates that some 60% of underprivileged children in the U.S. do not own a single book and that many school and public libraries are woefully under-stocked.

Based at Amherst College in Amherst, Massachusetts, RTR has been effective far beyond its small size. RTR provides books for students of all ages who don't otherwise have access to them. It does this by bringing books (without charge) to needy school and public libraries across the United States. This includes inner-city schools, poor rural towns, and Native American reservations.

To date, 2,000,000 books have been shipped to libraries, including 1,200,000 books to school libraries devastated by Hurricane Katrina.

In addition, RTR operates mentoring programs where children from low-income families come together with college student reading mentors. For example the Navajo Program links Native American high school students with Amherst College reading mentors. The mentors travel to the Navajo Reservation and work one-on-one with students and, in turn, the Native American students are able to travel to Amherst College to get an idea of college experience and to learn about a wide variety of career options from scientists, doctors, lawyers, writers, and artists.

RTR has gotten rave reviews and thanks from librarians all over the country. The organization is supported by individual donations as well as by prominent organizations such as Bank of America, Barnes and Noble, Comcast, DaimlerChrysler, Office Depot, Random House, Reuters, Robert F. Kennedy Memorial Fund, Target Stores, U.S. Airways, Verizon, and Xerox Corporation.

Reader To Reader (RTR), continued

RTR uses funding approximately as follows: program expenses, 83%, administrative expenses, 17%, 0% fundraising expenses.

For further information on making a monetary or book donation, or doing a book drive:

Website: www.readertoreader.org

Address: c/o Cadigan Center, 38 Woodside Ave., Amherst, MA 01002

Telephone: 413-256-8595

Email: dmazor@readertoreader.org

PICK ONE
HOW TO HELP PROMOTE
EDUCATION — THE NATION

Reading Is Fundamental (RIF)

When Margaret McNamara presented the boys she was tutoring a used book and said each boy could keep one, they were delighted. That led to her discovery that none of them had ever owned a book. That was in 1966 in Washington, D.C. and it was the inspiration that formed the organization called Reading Is Fundamental.

That led to book distribution projects in the public schools of Washington, D.C. and spread until, in 1975, the U.S. Congress passed legislation to create the Inexpensive Book Distribution Program. The legislation provided for matching funds for RIF's national book program.

Today, the U.S. Department of Education, several corporations, foundations and community organizations, with the support of thousands of individual donors and volunteers, all help support RIF's programs. These programs operate in all 50 states plus the District of Columbia, Guam, Puerto Rico and the U.S. Virgin Islands.

RIF programs distribute books to libraries, schools, childcare facilities, domestic shelters and even migrant camps, focusing especially on children at risk of educational failure.

RIF is now the oldest and largest nonprofit literacy organization in the United States.

Operating at some 21,000 sites, RIF provides five million children with about 17 million free books each year. The organization also offers programs for family literacy and older students mentoring younger children in reading.

Reading Is Fundamental (RIF), continued

RIF uses funding approximately as follows: program expenses, 90%, administrative expenses, 7%, fundraising expenses, 3%.
For further information:
Website: www.rif.org
Address: 1825 Connecticut Avenue NW, Suite 400, Washington, DC 20009
Telephone: 202-536-3400
Email: development@rif.org

PICK ONE
HOW TO HELP PROMOTE
EDUCATION — THE NATION

World Affairs Councils of America (WACA)

Broadly speaking, the mission of WACA is to empower American citizens to participate in the national debate on global affairs from an informed position. WACA is the umbrella, nonprofit organization that coordinates 87 nonprofit, nonpartisan, local councils, all of which are open to everyone who wishes to join.

There are currently about half a million participants in the system, including 28 affiliate organizations (such as the U.S. Council on Foreign Relations, the Center for Strategic and International Studies, the International Law Institute, the National Geographic Society, the U.S. State Department, etc.). WACA programs and educational services reach over 20 million people each year through forums, radio and TV, and school events.

WACA's Great Decisions program helps educate citizens about vital world affairs issues and provides them with the information to effectively participate in debates on policy. Great Decisions is the largest grassroots educational program in the country, with some 350,000 participants nationwide. In addition to its use by WACA local councils, this program is used by college campuses and high schools, by chapters of the League of Women Voters, and by thousands of small discussion groups.

Polls taken by reliable pollsters continue to demonstrate that, overall, the American electorate is woefully uninformed about important issues that effect us all. WACA is the largest and one of the most effective of the organizations that are working to correct this.

World Affairs Councils of America (WACA), continued

WACA National uses funding approximately as follows: program expenses, 90%, administrative expenses, 7%, fundraising expenses, 3%.

For further information:

See website Directory for Regional Councils:
www.worldaffairsdc.org/world-affairs-councils.php

National HQ Website: www.worldaffairscouncils.org

National Address: 1726 M Street NW, Suite 202,
    Washington, D.C. 20036

Telephone: 202-833-4557

Fax: 202-833-4555

Email: waca@worldaffairscouncils.org

PICK ONE
HOW TO HELP PROMOTE
EDUCATION — THE NATION

Donors Choose (DC)

Individual teachers describe specific projects that are needed for their classroom. Donors can choose projects from a wide variety of categories including by grade level, type of public school, location, subject (math, art, reading, etc.), and kind of resource needed (pencils, books, physical education equipment, drawing materials, etc.).

Teachers in *all* public schools in the U.S. are eligible to submit projects for funding.

Cost range of projects is typically $50 to $1000. Donors can fund all or any part of a project. Minimum donation is $10. For every project listed, amount funded to-date is shown.

A fulfillment fee of 15-25% is added to the project cost for shipping supplies to the school, monitoring the project, creating feedback info to the donor, etc. If the donor declines to fund the fulfillment fee, Doners Choose will fund it.

DC uses funding approximately as follows:
Program expenses, 86.5%, administrative expenses, 7.5%, fundraising expenses, 6%.
For further information:
Website: www.donorschoose.org
Address: 347 West 36th Street, Suite 503, New York, NY 10018
Telephone: 212-239-3615
Fax: 212-239-3619
Email: zwalker@donorschose.org

PICK ONE
HOW TO HELP PROMOTE
EDUCATION — THE NATION

United Way (UW)

UW is a national network of nearly 1,300 local organizations that work to advance the common good by focusing on education, income and health. United Way of America is the national organization that coordinates and assists the local chapters. Local chapters focus on the building blocks of a quality education that leads to a stable job, enough income to support a family through retirement, and good health. The chapters bring together people in local government, business, faith groups, nonprofits, the labor movement, and ordinary citizens to tackle the issues.

Education plays a dominant role in the activities of local chapters, which include providing funding, advocating policy improvements in schools, promoting budgets and programs that improve children's lives, and galvanizing communities to raise awareness of early learning. UW's "Success By 6" coalitions are proving to be highly effective throughout the U.S. And more than 660 UW chapters and their partners are carrying out the "Born Learning" public engagement campaign that helps parents, caregivers and communities support early learning.

United Ways are funding mentoring programs and after-school initiatives, putting volunteers in classrooms and supporting dropout prevention programs. And to ensure that children get early exposure to books, local chapters are promoting and funding books and literacy programs.

All in all, United Way chapters are among the most effective organizations for improving all aspects of local education.

While most contributions to UW are made through payroll deduction plans, donors can make individual contributions and can specify how their donations are used. Only 1% of donations go to help maintain the national organization-the rest is directed by volunteers to local needs.

United Way (UW), continued

The national UW organization uses its funding approximately as follows: program expenses, 89%, administrative expenses, 10%, fundraising expenses, 1%.

For further information:

To locate your local United Way, enter your zip code on the national website.

National website: www.liveunited.org

Address: 701 N. Fairfax St., Alexandria, VA 22314

Telephone: 703-836-7100

Email: del.galloway@uwa.unitedway.org

PICK ONE
HOW TO PROMOTE
WOMEN'S RIGHTS — THE NATION

National Partnership for Women and Families (NPWF)

Founded in 1971 and originally called the Women's Legal Defense Fund (WLDF), NPWF has become one of the nation's most effective advocates for women and families. To quote the organization, "Our goal is to create a society that is free, fair, and just. Where nobody has to experience discrimination, all workplaces are family-friendly, and no family is without quality, affordable health care and real economic security."

From outlawing sexual harassment to prohibiting pregnancy discrimination, from providing employees medical leave to protecting women's reproductive rights, NPWF has been at the forefront of every major advancement for women and their families.

In the years since its inception, it has led the fight to overhaul federal child support legislation. It has launched numerous outreach programs and lobbied for equal pay for equal work. It played a leading role in the enactment of laws against discrimination in the workplace because of medical conditions. In 1993 the organization won enactment of landmark legislation that requires employers to offer workers leave for childbirth, caregiving or medical emergencies. In 2005, NPWF led the coalition that won enactment of patient safety laws.

These are just a few of NPWF's many successes over 36 years in advocating for a free, fair, and just society.

National Partnership for Women and Families
(NPWF), continued

NPWF uses funding approximately as follows:
program expenses, 87%, administrative expenses, 5%,
fundraising expenses, 8%.
For further information:
Website: www.nationalpartnership.org
Address: 1875 Connecticut Avenue, NW, Suite 650,
    Washington, DC 20009
Telephone: 202-986-2600
Fax: 202-986-2539
Email: info@nationalpartnership.org

PICK ONE
HOW TO PROMOTE
WOMEN'S RIGHTS — THE NATION

Center for Reproductive Rights (CRR)

CRR is a leading legal advocacy organization that defends women's reproductive rights by using international human rights law and U.S. constitutional law to advance the reproductive freedom of women.

CRR believes reproductive freedom is one of the basic tenets of human dignity, self-determination, and equality embodied in the UN's Universal Declaration of Human Rights. And that the Universal Declaration of Human Rights needs strong law that will, in the end, determine if women are free to decide whether and when to have children; whether they will have access to contraception, health care, abortion and safe pregnancy care; and whether they will be able to make reproduction choices without coercion.

The organization has a record of success in strengthening and defining the course of reproductive rights law with positive outcomes in many U.S. court cases, including two landmark cases in the Supreme Court.

CRR has worked to improve the right to a private doctor-patient relationship; the elimination of harmful practices such as female genital mutilation; access to reproductive health care for women facing economic or social barriers; and protecting reproductive health workers from violence and coercion.

Center for Reproductive Rights (CRR), continued

CRR uses funding approximately as follows:
program expenses, 77%, administrative expenses, 8%,
fundraising expenses, 15%.
For further information:
Website: www.reproductiverights.org
Address: 120 Wall St., 14th Fl., New York, NY 10005
Telephone: 917-637-3671
Fax: 917-637-3666
Email: contribute@reprorights.org

PICK ONE
HOW TO PROMOTE
WOMEN'S RIGHTS — THE NATION

Family Violence Prevention Fund (FVPF)

FVPF works to end violence against women and children, to assist those who are victims of violence, and to educate individuals and communities on how to mitigate and ultimately end the devastating effects of violence.

The organization was instrumental in developing and achieving passage of the Violence Against Women Act passed by Congress in 1994. It continues to have outreach programs to parents and children, police, prosecutors, judges, health care providers, employers, and others to ensure that violence prevention efforts are meaningful and self-sustaining.

FVPF works with domestic violence programs, batterer intervention programs, family and juvenile courts, responsible fatherhood groups, supervised visitation centers, and community organizers to form collaborations that promote family safety.

Immigrant and refugee women also face challenges to safety in the U.S.

FVPF has helped to develop services and protective laws in these areas and some progress has been made. But there are many problems still to overcome, especially the issue of intimate partner violence.

FVPF administers the national program of the Robert Wood Johnson Foundation to create and support community-based models whose goal is to increase positive relationship skills among 10- to 14-year-olds.

FVPF, along with other organizations, has been concerned that some personnel of the Family Court System in the U.S. have lacked the skills necessary to fairly and competently adjudicate domestic violence cases. In 1998, a partnership of FVPF, the National Council of Juvenile and Family Court Judges, and the

U.S. Department of Justice was formed to offer domestic violence workshops for judges and other judicial officers, and since that time good progress has been made.

FVPF uses funding approximately as follows: program expenses, 84.5%, administrative expenses, 7%, fundraising expenses, 8.5%.

For further information:

Website: www/endabuse.org

Address: 383 Rhode Island S, Ste. 304, San Francisco, CA 94103

Telephone: 415-252-8900

Fax: 415-252-8991

Email: info@endabuse.org

PICK ONE
HOW TO PROMOTE
WOMEN'S RIGHTS — THE NATION

Tahirih Justice Center (TJC)

TJC was founded in 1997 to provide legal services for refugee and immigrant women who have fled to the U.S. after having undergone human rights abuses. The TJC is named after a 19th century woman of the Bahai faith who fought for the freedom and equality of women in Persia and was martyred for her then-radical views.

TJC has provided direct legal, social, and medical services for some 6000 abused women. To serve the ever-increasing number of women in need, TJC makes extensive use of volunteer attorneys, doctors, nurses, and social service professionals. Their public advocacy and their fight to establish women's rights resulted in legal victories that set a national precedent and revolutionized asylum law in the United States.

The efficiency and effectiveness of this organization was recognized by winning the 2007 Washington Post Award for Excellence in Nonprofit Management.

TJC uses funding approximately as follows:
program expenses, 94%, administrative expenses, 3%,
fundraising expenses, 3%.
For further information:
Website: www.tahirih.org
Address: 6066 Leesburg Pike, #220, Falls Church,
VA 22041
Telephone: 703-575-0070
Fax: 703-575-0069
Email: justice@tahirih.org

PICK ONE
HOW TO HELP VETERANS AND
ACTIVE ARMED FORCES
PERSONNEL — THE NATION

United Service Organizations (USO)

Since 1941, USO has been a congressionally chartered, nonprofit organization that is not a part of the federal government. Its mission has always remained the same: to provide morale, welfare, and recreation-type services to service members and their families.

Services include free Internet and e-mail access, libraries and reading rooms, housing assistance, family crisis counseling, support groups, game rooms, and nursery facilities.

The USO currently operates more than 130 centers worldwide, including mobile canteens located in the continental United States and overseas. Overseas centers are located in Germany, Italy, the United Arab Emirates, Japan, Qatar, Korea, Afghanistan, Guam, and Kuwait. Service members and their families visit USO centers more than 5 million times each year. USO celebrity entertainment tours bring volunteer celebrities to entertain, lift morale, and express the gratitude and support of the American people. Currently, more than 25,000 volunteers lend their time and talents to the USO.

USO relies on the generosity of individuals and corporations to support USO activities.

United Service Organizations (USO), continued

USO uses funding approximately as follows:
program expenses, 89%, administrative expenses, 4%,
fundraising expenses, 7%.
For further information:
Website: www.uso.org
Address: 2111 Wilson Boulevard, Suite 1200,
    Arlington, VA 22201
Telephone: 800-876-7469
Address for donations: Department WS, P.O. Box
    96860, Washington, DC 20090
Email: info@uso.org

Pick One
How to Help Veterans and Active Armed Forces Personnel — The Nation

Armed Services YMCA of the USA (ASYMCA)

(a sectarian organization)

ASYMCA is the oldest military assistance organization in the U.S., having been founded in 1861 during the Civil War. Today it is the nation's leading nonprofit organization that provides support to junior enlisted personnel and their families. Sanctioned by the Department of Defense and with the aid of private donations and a corps of more than 9000 volunteers, ASYMCA helps some 400,000 military families each year.

The organization helps the families of individuals that serve our country by providing a host of services such as helping spouses learn life skills, care for children, help with medical expenses, food services, and even make ends meet. ASYMCA also helps comfort and educate young minds, helping them understand and cope with the absence of a parent.

ASYMCA has received high ratings from the charity rating services for its efficiency and effectiveness, and in general for promoting strong military families, strong children, and communities that support them.

ASYMCA uses funding approximately as follows: program expenses, 87%, administrative expenses, 8%, fundraising expenses, 5%.

For further information:

Website: www.asymca.org

Address: 6359 Walker Lane, Suite 200, Alexandria, VA 22310

Telephone: 800-597-1260

Fax: 703-313-9668

Email: ssimms@asymca.org

PICK ONE
HOW TO HELP VETERANS AND
ACTIVE ARMED FORCES
PERSONNEL — THE NATION

Fisher House Foundation (FHF)

FHF offers a number of services for families of active military personnel and veterans beyond that provided by the Departments of Defense and Veterans Affairs. Foremost among these services are the Fisher Houses that are available at all major military medical centers. Because families often have to travel great distances from their homes to receive specialized medical care, FHF donates homes at medical facilities to enable family members to be close to a loved one undergoing treatment. FHF provides lodging for more than 10,000 families each year, and *there is no charge to any family* to stay at a Fisher House.

Among additional FHF services is the Hero Miles Program. In coordination with airlines, passengers can donate their frequent flyer miles to FHF. The organization then produces free airline tickets for military men and women (and their families) to and from a military or VA medical center for treatment related to service in Iraq or Afghanistan.

FHF provides numerous other support services including the Scholarships for Military Children Program, and the Caring Bridge Program which enables military families to create their own, free website in order to let relatives and friends know the latest news about a service person's treatment and status.

Working closely with the DOD and VA, Fisher House Foundation has received the very highest ratings from the major charity rating organizations for its efficiency and effectiveness.

Fisher House Foundation (FHF), continued

FHF uses funding approximately as follows:
program expenses, 95%, administrative expenses, 2%,
fundraising expenses, 3%.
For further information:
Website: www.fisherhouse.org
Address: 1401 Rockville Pike, Ste.600, Rockville,
    MD 20852
Telephone: 888-294-8560
Fax: 877-294-8562
Email: info@fisherhouse.org

PICK ONE
HOW TO HELP VETERANS AND ACTIVE ARMED FORCES PERSONNEL — THE NATION

National Military Family Association (NMFA)

Originally created in 1969 as the National Military Wives Association, the organization broadened its services in 1948 to all family members of service personnel and changed its name to NMFA. Since then, NMFA has been one of the leading advocates for improvements in the quality of military family life.

NMFA board members and officers receive no compensation, and the organization operates with the help of large numbers of volunteers.

NMFA acts as an advocacy group for military families. It advises several Department of Defense agencies and testifies before Congressional Committees on current family needs. It has successfully lobbied to improve family medical benefits, education for dependents, relocation reimbursement, spousal employment opportunities, and retiree and survivor benefits.

Among its other services, NMFA sponsors a military spouse scholarship program, a family health care program, and recreational camps for children of deployed service members. It also operates a resource center that provides information on everything from housing to commissary food discounts.

This organization has received the very highest ratings from the major charity rating organizations.

National Military Family Association (NMFA),
continued

NMFA uses funding approximately as follows:
program expenses, 81.5%, administrative expenses,
8.5%, fundraising expenses, 10%.
For further information:
Website: www.nmfa.org
Address: 2500 N. Van Dorn St., Ste.102, Alexandria,
VA 22302
Telephone: 800-260-0218
Fax: 703-931-4600
Email: families@nmfa.org

Pick One
How to Help Protect
the Environment — The Nation

Environmental Defense Fund (EDF)

Scientists founded Environmental Defense Fund 40 years ago, linking science, economics, and law to create solutions to society's most urgent environmental problems. With more than 500,000 members, they have become one of the leading organizations that promote a broad range of environmental protection.

EDF focuses on four areas: climate, ecosystems, oceans, and health. The climate effort fights global warming by reducing emissions of carbon dioxide and other greenhouse gases. Ecosystem work focuses on protecting land, water, and wildlife. The oceans program develops market incentives to revive fisheries and fishing communities, setting standards for sustainable seafood and expanding marine protected areas. Health efforts focus on cutting air pollution from smokestacks and tailpipes and reducing human exposure to toxic chemicals.

To mention a few of its many accomplishments, EDF was the primary player to win the U.S. ban on DDT. It played a major role in convincing federal regulators to phase the lead out of gasoline and to eliminate CFC's that damage the earth's ozone layer. The federal government used EDF's design to create the Clean Air Act. Their cap-and-trade plan to mitigate global warming became the program adopted by the Kyoto treaty. It played a key role in creating the world's largest marine reserve in Hawaii. And its campaign against toxic air pollution blocked the new construction of dirty coal plants.

Environmental Defense Fund (EDF), continued

EDF uses funding approximately as follows:
program expenses, 79%, administrative expenses, 5%,
fundraising expenses, 16%.
For further information:
Website: www.edf.org
Address: 257 Park Avenue South, New York,
    NY 10010
Telephone: 800-684-3322
Email: members@environmentaldefense.org

PICK ONE
HOW TO HELP PROTECT
THE ENVIRONMENT — THE NATION

Natural Resources Defense Council (NRDC)

Founded in 1970, NRDC has become one of the nation's most effective environmental action groups, combining the grassroots power of 1.2 million members and online activists with the courtroom clout and expertise of more than 350 lawyers, scientists, and other professionals. Its purpose is to safeguard the Earth, its people, its plants and animals, and the natural systems on which all life depends. Because NRDC operates both in the U.S. and abroad, it is listed here and in the category of Environmentalism Worldwide.

NRDC works to solve the most pressing environmental issues we face today, including curbing global warming, getting toxic chemicals out of the environment, moving America beyond oil, reviving our oceans, saving wildlife and wild places, and helping China go green. Programs include teaming up with corporations to promote energy efficiency and environmentally responsible production practices, protecting forests and endangered ecosystems from development, and encouraging natural resource protection through the expansion of wildlife and marine reserves.

NRDC strives to protect nature in ways that advance the long-term welfare of present and future generations but also to foster the fundamental right of all people to have a voice in decisions that affect their environment.

Worth Magazine has named NRDC one of America's 100 best charities and *The New York Times* calls it, "One of the nation's most powerful environmental groups."

Natural Resources Defense Council (NRDC), continued

NRDC uses funding as follows: program expenses, 80%, administrative expenses, 8%, fund raising expenses, 12%.
For further information:
Website: www.nrdc.org
Address: 40 West 20th Street, New York, NY 10011
Telephone: 212-727-2700
Fax: 212-727-1773
Email: membership@nrdc.org

Pick One
How to Help Protect
the Environment — The Nation

The Nature Conservancy (TNC)

TNC is probably the largest conservation organization in the world. Its stated purpose is: "to preserve the plants, animals and natural communities that represent the diversity of life on Earth by protecting the lands and waters they need to survive."

It addresses threats to natural land and marine ecosystems from development, fire, climate change, invasive species, overgrazing, unsustainable farming, etc. It accomplishes this by purchases, exchanges, partnerships, management agreements, and conservation easements.

Since 1951 more than 117 million acres of land and 5,000 miles of rivers have been protected worldwide. TNC has been involved in everything from grasslands to coral reefs, and it currently operates more than 100 marine conservation projects. With more than one million members, the organization works in all 50 states and in more than 30 countries.

The key to all of these successful conservation projects is applying sound science with market-based solutions and partnering with government agencies, businesses, international institutions, and other nonprofit organizations.

TNC has developed a strategic planning process called *Conservation by Design* which identifies the highest priority landscapes and seascapes that need protection; places that have the best chance of ensuring continuing biodiversity. The organization's goal is no less than securing the future of the natural world.

The Nature Conservancy (TNC), continued

TNC uses funding approximately as follows:
program expenses, 80%, administrative expenses,
12%, fundraising expenses, 8%.
For further information:
Website: www.nature.org
Address: 4245 N Fairfax Dr, Ste. 100, Arlington,
    VA 22203
Telephone: 800-628-6860
Email: membership@tnc.org

Pick One
How to Help Protect
the Environment — The Nation

Rainforest Alliance (RA)

Founded in 1987, the goal of RA is to conserve biodiversity and encourage sustainable livelihoods by making farming, forestry, and tourism environmentally sound and economically productive.

RA works with everyone from large, multinational corporations to small, community cooperatives to set standards that bring responsibly produced products to market. The organization sets standards that conserve natural ecosystems and wildlife and that promote economic progress and the welfare of workers and their communities. Farms and forestry businesses that meet these standards receive the Rainforest Alliance Certified™ seal.

In North America, RA focuses primarily on the responsible management of forestlands by working with forestry companies and logging operations. RA also works with paper products companies, furniture manufacturers, and others who use wood products to choose sources that produce wood and pulp responsibly.

Across the U.S. the Rainforest Alliance has a broad outreach program to educate architects, builders, printers, and others about the benefits of procuring materials that have been sustainably produced. RA also has an outreach program to inform consumers about products from green companies.

The Rainforest Alliance also operates several other programs, including: For teachers, lessons, presentations, stories and articles, etc., that help connect students to conservation. The Eco-Exchange program offers reporters, other conservation groups, foundations and government agencies news about the latest environmental issues and successful projects.

Rainforest Alliance (RA), continued

RA uses funding approximately as follows:
program expenses, 93%, administrative expenses, 2%,
fundraising expenses, 5%.
For further information:
Website: www.rainforest-alliance.org
Address: 665 Broadway, Ste.500, New York,
    NY 10012
Telephone: 888-693-2784
Fax: 212-677-2187
Email: development@ra.org

PICK ONE
HOW TO HELP PROTECT
THE ENVIRONMENT — THE NATION

Rocky Mountain Institute (RMI)

Established in 1982, Rocky Mountain Institute is an applied research organization that advises governments, businesses, communities, and individuals on the efficient and sustainable use of natural resources. It does this through the focus on Natural Capitalism, a new and rapidly spreading business model that harnesses sound environmental performance as an engine of competitive advantage. Natural Capitalism shows these kinds of groups how to create more wealth and employment by doing what they do more efficiently.

RMI has created ideas and models that have reframed the debates on climate change, energy production, transportation and water usage, to name a few. The organization has developed pioneering strategies for self-sustaining communities, clean energy systems based on hydrogen, and new engineering and architectural techniques that dramatically improve the human, environmental, and financial performance of buildings.

In all its work, RMI is independent and non-adversarial, with a strong emphasis on market-based solutions that at the same time sustain and restore a healthy environment.

Rocky Mountain Institute (RMI), continued

RMI uses funding as follows: program expenses, 73%, administrative expenses, 19%, fundraising expenses, 8%.

For further information:

Website: www.rmi.org

Address: 2317 Snowmass Creek Rd, Snowmass,
　　CO 81654

Telephone: 970-927-3851

Fax: 970-927-4510

Email: outreach@rmi.org

PICK ONE
HOW TO PROMOTE RENEWABLE ENERGY AND GREEN TECHNOLOGY — THE NATION

Center for Resource Solutions (CRS)

Founded in 1997, the goal of CRS was to provide the necessary leadership to increase the demand and use of renewable energy around the world. Now, although CRS is a relatively small organization, it has a big impact. It creates innovative environmental policies and consumer protection mechanisms for renewable energy, energy efficiency, and greenhouse gas reductions that are used nationally and around the world.

CRS sponsors international meetings between energy policy-makers around the world. It has an important role, in cooperation with Australia, Canada, Mexico, and the International Energy Agency (IEA), in developing global energy policies. CRS has been a key player in helping to create China's Sustainable Energy Program.

Through its *Green-e* logo, CRS has created the leading voluntary program in the U.S. that certifies that renewable energy projects meet sound environmental standards. The organization's *Green-e Climate* program certifies that greenhouse gas reduction projects (offsets) are legitimate. The *Green-e Marketplace* logo establishes that businesses and other organizations have achieved renewable energy excellence.

Overall, CRS has been a major contributor to the development and use of renewable energy throughout the world.

In addition to individual donations, CRS is partially supported by the U.S. Department of Energy, the Environmental Protection Agency, the National Park Service, as well as many corporations and foundations.

Center for Resource Solutions (CRS), continued

CRS uses funding approximately as follows:
program expenses, 78%, administrative expenses,
18%, fundraising expenses, 4%.
For further information:
Website: www.resource-solutions.org
Mailing Address: PO Box 29512, San Francisco,
   CA 94129
Headquarters Address: Presidio Bldg, Arguello at
   Moraga, San Francisco, CA 94129
Telephone: 415-561-2100
Fax: 415-561-2105
Email: info@resource-solutions.org

PICK ONE
HOW TO PROMOTE RENEWABLE ENERGY AND GREEN TECHNOLOGY — THE NATION

Resources for the Future (RFF)

Founded in 1952, RFF conducts independent research on environmental, natural resource, and energy issues. It has brought together under one roof a unique community of scholars whose work enables policymakers to make sound choices.

The organization has been a leader in the application of economics to the use and conservation of natural resources. Its scholars develop innovative and practical solutions for such areas as climate change, renewable energy, pollution control, land and water use, biodiversity, hazardous waste, transportation policy, and ecosystem management.

RFF economics researchers are deeply engaged in developing solutions that limit the cost uncertainties of reducing greenhouse gas emissions and adapting to a changing climate. Other staff members develop ways to measure the benefits of forest and fisheries management, agricultural systems, and water resources.

The organization is a leader in determining the benefits and losses due to environmental regulations, and the development of new and alternative approaches to regulation.

Other areas of RFF's research include innovative approaches to reduce air pollution from cars and other modes of transportation, reduce fuel use, and reduce traffic congestion.

RFF has earned a reputation for research and analysis of the highest order. It shares its work with government policymakers at all levels, environmental organizations, business groups, and the media. RFF neither lobbies nor takes a position on legislative or regulatory proposals; its purpose is strictly to provide informed advice.

Resources for the Future (RFF), continued

RFF uses funding approximately as follows:
program expenses, 80.5%, administrative expenses,
14.5%, fundraising expenses, 5%.
For further information:
Website: www.rff.org
Address: 1616 P Sreet NW, Washington, D.C. 20036
Telephone: 202-328-5016
Fax: 202-939-3460
Email: info@rff.org

PICK ONE
HOW TO CONTROL IMMIGRATION
AND POPULATION GROWTH
THE NATION

Numbers USA

Its full name is Numbers USA Education and Research Foundation. It is a nonprofit, nonpartisan immigration-reduction organization of 450,000+ members that conducts research on the impacts of high numerical levels of immigration and educates the public, opinion leaders, and policy makers on the results of these and other studies. The organization bases its work on the belief that environmental sustainability, economic justice, the rule of law, and individual liberty are threatened by massive U.S. population growth.

Numbers USA asserts that current immigration flows are wildly higher than the U.S. immigration tradition that nurtured America during most of its history. Traditional flows averaged around 250,000 a year from 1776–1976. Since 1990, around 1 million legal immigrants a year and more than 800,000 illegal immigrants a year settle permanently in the U.S.

Numbers USA tracks the effect of population growth on a wide variety of issues, including joblessness, amnesty for illegal aliens, immigration enforcement, birthright citizenship, environment, worker visas, in-state tuition, medical treatment, urban sprawl, effect on businesses, and future projections.

Numbers USA uses funding approximately as follows: program expenses, 90%, administrative expenses, 7%, fundraising expenses, 3%
For further information:
Website: www.usanumbers.org
Address: 1601 N. Kent St. #1100, Arlington, VA 22209
Telephone: 877-885-7733
Email: anne@numbersusa.com

PICK ONE
HOW TO CONTROL IMMIGRATION
AND POPULATION GROWTH
THE NATION

Federation for American Immigration Reform (FAIR)

Founded in 1979, FAIR is a leading organization for reforming U.S. immigration by improving border security, stopping illegal immigration, and promoting reasonable immigration levels. With more than 250,000 members and supporters, FAIR is a non-partisan organization whose members range from liberals to conservatives. Its grassroots networks enable citizens to speak up for immigration policies that are in the nation's best interests.

The organization produces research and publications that are used by government officials to prepare new legislation. National and international media regularly utilize FAIR as a source for the latest information and thinking on immigration. And FAIR, more than any other organization in America, has been called to testify before Congress on immigration bills.

With more than one million legal and illegal immigrants settling in the U.S. each year, immigration is having a significant impact on health care, education, the environment, crime, etc. FAIR advocates a temporary moratorium on all immigration except spouses and minor children of U.S. citizens, and a limited number of refugees. In the interim, we need to regain control of our borders and then reduce overall immigration to the more traditional level of 300,000 per year.

In many recent polls, Americans agree that the era of mass migration to the U.S. as a means of solving problems of poverty and overpopulation in other countries needs to end, and that these problems must be solved where people live rather than continuing to export them to the United States.

Federation for American Immigration Reform (FAIR), continued

FAIR uses funding approximately as follows: program expenses, 74%, administrative expenses, 13%, fundraising expenses, 13%.
For further information:
Website: www.fairus.org
Address: 25 Massachusetts Avenue, Suite 330,
    Washington, DC 20001
Telephone: 877-627-3247
Fax: 202-387-3447
Email: membership@fairus.org

PICK ONE
HOW TO CONTROL IMMIGRATION AND POPULATION GROWTH
THE NATION

Negative Population Growth (NPG)

NPG is an organization of some 30,000 members, founded in 1972, working to achieve long-term sustainability by gradually stabilizing population size of the U.S. at around 150 to 200 million (its size 50 years ago, which scientists agree was optimal for its resources). NPG believes an optimal world population is between two and three billion.

The organization claims that only with a much smaller population can fragile ecosystems conserve finite resources and ensure that future generations will inherit a clean and healthy environment where all Americans can enjoy a quality standard of living. To this end, NPG promotes concepts such as reducing the fertility rate to 1.5 births per woman, and reducing the level of immigration into the U.S. from 1.5 million per year to between 100,000 and 200,000.

NPG is one of the few organizations to publicly advocate the development of a steady state economy, going against traditional policy that claims constant economic growth is necessary.

And NPG is unique among national organizations in calling for a turnaround in population growth and describing the means to achieve it.

NPG uses funding approximately as follows: program expenses, 82%, administrative expenses, 10%, fundraising expenses, 8%.

For more information:

Website: www.npg.org

Address: 2861 Duke St., Suite 36, Alexandria, VA 22314

Telephone: 703-370-9310

Fax: 703-370-9514

Email: npg@npg.org

PICK ONE
HOW TO PROTECT ANIMAL RIGHTS
AND WILDLIFE — THE NATION

Animal Legal Defense Fund (ALDF)

For more than a quarter-century, ALDF has been fighting to protect the lives and advance the interests of animals through the legal system. Founded in 1979 by attorneys active in shaping the emerging field of animal law, ALDF has blazed the trail for stronger enforcement of anti-cruelty laws and more humane treatment of animals in every corner of American life. Today, ALDF's groundbreaking efforts to push the U.S. legal system to end the suffering of abused animals are supported by hundreds of dedicated attorneys and more than 100,000 members. Every day, ALDF works to protect animals by:

- Filing groundbreaking lawsuits to stop animal abuse and expand the boundaries of animal law.
- Providing free legal assistance to prosecutors handling cruelty cases.
- Working to strengthen state anti-cruelty statutes.
- Encouraging the federal government to enforce existing animal protection laws.
- Providing public education through seminars, workshops and other outreach efforts.

ALDF's primary programs include their Litigation Program which files cutting-edge lawsuits to stop the abuse of companion animals, and animals abused in industries including factory farming and the entertainment business; the Criminal Justice Program which works with law enforcement and prosecutors to seek maximum penalties for animal abusers; and, the Animal Law Program, dedicated to fostering the field of animal law among legal professionals and in law schools nationwide.

Animal Legal Defense Fund (ALDF), continued

ALDF uses funding approximately as follows:
program expenses, 81%, administrative expenses, 4%,
fundraising expenses, 15%.
For further information:
Website: www.aldf.org
Address: 170 East Cotati Ave., Cotati, CA 94931
Telephone: 707-795-2538
Fax: 707-795-7280
Email: info@aldf.org

PICK ONE
HOW TO PROTECT ANIMAL RIGHTS
AND WILDLIFE — THE NATION

American Society for the Prevention of Cruelty to Animals (ASPCA)

ASPCA has a long history. It was founded way back in 1866 as the first organization in the U.S. to alleviate the suffering of animals and was the first organization to be granted legal authority to investigate crimes against animals and to make arrests. In years past the fledgling organization forced owners to stop whipping horses, removed overworked dogs from industrial treadmills, forced improvements in slaughterhouses, and a host of other gains. To this day the ASPCA saves pets from abuse, rescues endangered animals, promotes healthy animal shelters, works to end abusive factory farming, and provides the expertise to pass humane laws, to name a few of its activities. The organization's goal is no less than to see the day when no animal will live in pain or fear.

Among its many activities, ASPCA operates an around-the-clock poison control center; offers expert animal training advice; works with cities to end unnecessary euthanasia; prepares disaster readiness plans for animal safety; partners with animal shelters across the country to improve adoption rates; provides forensics experts to help investigate and prosecute crimes against animals; has a strong public outreach program; and lobbies policymakers to pass enlightened humane laws.

American Society for the Prevention of Cruelty to Animals (ASPCA), continued

ASPCA uses funding approximately as follows: program expenses, 82%, administrative expenses, 2%, fundraising expenses, 16%.
For further information:
Website: www.aspca.org
Address: 424 East 92nd Street, New York, NY 10128
Telephone: 800-628-0028
Fax: 212-423-9813
Email: development@aspca.org

Pick One
How to Protect Animal Rights and Wildlife — The Nation

People for the Ethical Treatment of Animals (PETA)

Founded in 1980, PETA is the largest animal rights organization in the world, with some 1.8 million members worldwide. PETA believes that animals feel pain, pleasure, fear, frustration, loneliness, and motherly love, and that whenever we consider doing something that would interfere with their needs, we are morally obligated to take these feelings into account. They insist that animals have an inherent worth—a value completely separate from their usefulness to humans. They believe that every creature with a will to live has a right to live free from pain and suffering, and that animals do not exist solely for human use.

PETA establishes and defends the rights of all animals and focuses especially on four areas in the U.S.: factory farming, laboratory experimentation and testing, the fur trade, and the entertainment industry. It also campaigns against cockfighting, bullfighting, fishing, and the consumption of meat.

PETA employs a broad range of activities, including cruelty investigations, animal rescue, animal rights legislation, research on alternatives to abusive animal testing, protest campaigns, spay and neuter programs, etc.

It organizes grassroots educational campaigns that encourage respectful treatment of animals and promote alternatives to every abusive animal use. PETA has carried out several protest campaigns to change the behavior of specific industries and commercial operations. (For example, it succeeded in pressuring McDonalds to change the way their suppliers treat chickens.)

People for the Ethical Treatment of Animals (PETA),
continued

PETA uses funding approximately as follows:
program expenses, 84%, administrative expenses, 4%,
fundraising expenses, 12%.
For further information:
Website: www.peta.org
Address: 501 Front St., Norfolk, VA 23510
Telephone: 757-622-7382
Fax: 757-628-0786
Email: donations@peta.org

PICK ONE
HOW TO PROTECT ANIMAL RIGHTS
AND WILDLIFE — THE NATION

Wildlife Conservation Society (WCS)

Founded in 1895, WCS has worked to save wildlife and wild lands throughout the world. Their goal is to change attitudes toward nature so that people and wildlife can live in sustainable interaction on both a local and a global scale.

Led by their flagship Bronx Zoo, WCS manages the world's largest system of urban wildlife parks. By combining the resources of urban wildlife parks with field projects around the world, WCS helps sustain the planet's biodiversity and provides leadership in environmental education.

To sustain biodiversity, WCS helps protect wild landscapes in North America, Latin America, Africa, and Asia—53 countries in all—and has helped save countless species from tigers to butterflies. It does this through a combination of careful science and expert management in the field.

Another important part of the organization's work is its large outreach programs that provide environmental education to literally millions of people nationally and internationally.

WCS uses funding approximately as follows: program expenses, 85%, administrative expenses, 11%, fundraising expenses, 4%.
For further information:
Website: www.wcs.org
Address: 2300 Southern Blvd., Bronx, NY 10460
Telephone: 718-220-5100
Email: development@wcs.org

PICK ONE
HOW TO PROMOTE THE ARTS
THE NATION

The United States, with its thousands of national, regional, and local organizations dedicated to promoting arts and culture, is unique in all the world. It's beyond the scope of this book to include even a fraction of them. But here are three quite small charities that we believe are deserving of support, and two very, very large ones that can only be described as magnificent.

Academy of American Poets (AAP)

Founded in 1934, AAP promotes recognition and appreciation of contemporary poetry, and supports American poets at all stages of their careers.

Foremost among its many programs is National Poetry Month. Held each year in April, this event brings together thousands of libraries, schools, booksellers and book publishers, poetry clubs, and individual poets to celebrate poetry in American culture.

AAP maintains the Poetry Audio Archive, one of the world's finest collection of aural poetry records.

The organization provides free poetry lesson plans for high school teachers, publishes *American Poet* magazine, and presents the most important collection of poetry awards in the U.S. Its New York City based *Poets Forum* presents a series of readings and discussions with distinguished poets.

AAP's award-winning website gets a million visitors each month, and offers an abundance of content on contemporary American poetry.

Academy of American Poets (AAP), continued

AAP uses funding approximately as follows:
Program expenses, 77%, administrative expenses,
10.5%, fundraising expenses, 12.5%
For further information:
Website: www.poets.org
Address: 584 Broadway, Suite 604, New York,
    NY 10012
Telephone: 212-274-0343
Fax: 212-274-9427
Email: membership@poets.org

PICK ONE
HOW TO PROMOTE THE ARTS
THE NATION

International Sculpture Center (ISC)

Founded in 1960, the goal of ISC is to advance this art form and to expand the public understanding and appreciation of sculpture. It believes that the role of sculpture is not only to aesthetically please, but also to educate and effect social change.

ISC members include sculptors, curators, historians, educators, critics, galleries, museums, journalists, and foundries.

The organization publishes *Sculpture*, an international monthly magazine that addresses all forms of contemporary sculpture and includes technical information, criticisms and exploration of new materials and techniques. The members' edition of the magazine also contains employment information and news about commissions, grants, conferences, and other special events.

ISC maintains a database of sculptors, sculpture parks and gardens, and a directory of schools for students. It also describes educational programs for students and lists annual student awards competitions.

ISC uses funding approximately as follows: program expenses, 83%, administrative expenses, 14%, fundraising expenses, 3%.
For further information:
Website: www.sculpture.org
Address: 19-B Fairgrounds Rd., Hamilton, NJ 08619
Telephone: 609-689-1051
Fax: 609-689-1061.
Email: development@sculpture.org

PICK ONE
HOW TO PROMOTE THE ARTS
THE NATION

Meet the Composer (MTC)

Founded in 1974, MTC works to help composers by supporting the creation of new work, its performance, and distribution. It does this by furthering the collaboration between composers and performing artists and, over the years, working with thousands of civic groups to support a commitment to new music.

MTC focuses on dynamic interaction between audiences, musicians, and a living composer in the belief that all are stimulated and inspired by this process. The organization is now active in all fifty states, bringing a broad range of musical experiences to audiences across the country, including small towns, rural areas, suburbs, and inner cities.

Since 1974, MTC's programs have connected more than 6500 composers with audiences totaling some 45 million. This new music represents everything from classical to jazz to folk to experimental. As the nation's leading commissioner of new American music, MTC has helped composers to create more than 1400 new works over several decades.

And MTC has been a leader in promoting collaborations between composers and choreographers, having commissioned more than 300 cooperative works.

Meet the Composer (MTC), continued

MTC uses funding approximately as follows:
program expenses, 88.5%, administrative expenses,
7.5%, fundraising expenses, 4%.
For further information:
Website: www.meetthecomposer.org
Address: 90 John St., Ste. 312, New York, NY 10038
Telephone: 212-645-6949
Fax: 212-645-9669
Email: mtc@meetthecomposer.org

PICK ONE
HOW TO PROMOTE THE ARTS
THE NATION

John F. Kennedy Center for the Performing Arts

Located on 17 acres overlooking the Potomac River, each year the Kennedy Center is gathers the greatest artists from around the world and presents an unparalleled variety of theater, musicals, dance, orchestral, jazz, pops, folk, and multi-media performances that touch the lives of millions.

In addition to a full program in Washington D.C., the Center sponsors performances and related activities in all 50 states.

As a Presidential Memorial, the Kennedy Center receives federal funds for the operation and maintenance of the building only. No government funding goes toward performances or the Center's many educational activities. Ticket sales do not cover costs. The Center's activities are made possible by foundation and corporate donations, and a significant part of its budget is provided by individual donations which are absolutely critical to its mission. Individual donations help make possible

- The presentation of more than 3100 performances each year.
- The commission of new works of music, dance and theater.
- A public outreach to more than 11 million young people, in the form of school partnerships, teacher workshops, master classes, competitions for young musicians, dancers and actors, and special performances at schools.

Contributors and Kennedy Center members receive a host of special privileges.

John F. Kennedy Center for the Performing Arts,
continued

The Kennedy Center uses funding approximately as follows: program expenses, 86%, administrative expenses, 9%, fundraising expenses, 5%.
For further information:
Website: www.kennedy-center.org
Address: 2700 F St. NW, Washington, DC 20566
Telephone: 800-472-3556
Fax: 202-416-8076
Email: membership@kennedy-center.org

Pick One
How to Promote the Arts
The Nation

Lincoln Center for the Performing Arts (LCPA)

LCPA is one of the world's leading presenters of performing arts. It is one of 12 world-renowned organizations* that make up the Lincoln Center, which is the world's foremost performing arts center.

Each year LCPA itself offers more than 400 performances of music, opera, theater, dance, and multi-media events. These include the well-known series *American Songbook, Great Performers, Lincoln Center Festival, Lincoln Center Out of Doors, Midsummer Night Swing*, and the *Mostly Mozart Festival*. The programs run the gamut from opera performed with life-sized puppets to Japanese kabuki theater, Korean drumming, African dance and innovative video presentations. Many of the performance are free.

LCPA presents the popular TV series *Live From Lincoln Center* which enables millions of viewers to see some of the finest programs at the Lincoln Center. And its educational arm, the Lincoln Center Institute, serves more than 200,000 students across the country who are enrolled in grades K-12.

As significant as these activities are, LCPA has another responsibility that makes the Lincoln Center function. It is the manager of the entire Lincoln Center complex including all its companies in residence, coordinating such functions as maintenance, security, parking, and capital development.

LCPA is a nonprofit organization that receives less than 5% of its budget from government funding and 95% from private donations. Because LCPA manages all of the other prestigious organizations that make up the Lincoln Center, private donations to LCPA enable the entire Lincoln Center complex to continue to be the world's leading performing arts center.

LCPA thanks its members and donors with special privileges, discounts, and other benefits.

*The other organizations are: Chamber Music Society of Lincoln Center, Film Society of Lincoln Center, Jazz at Lincoln Center, Julliard School, Lincoln Center Theater, Metropolitan Opera, New York City Ballet, New York City Opera, New York Philharmonic, New York Public Library for the Performing Arts, School of American Ballet.

LCPA uses funding approximately as follows: program expenses, 85%, administrative expenses, 9%, fundraising expenses, 6%.
For further information:
Website: www.lincolncenter.org
Address: 70 Lincoln Center Plaza, New York,
    NY 10023
Telephone: 212-875-5443
Fax: 212-875-5468
Email: development@lincolncenter.org

PICK ONE
HOW TO PROMOTE GOOD
GOVERNMENT AND PROTECT
INDIVIDUAL RIGHTS — THE NATION

Common Cause (CC)

Founded in 1970, and now with more than 400,000 members and supporters, CC is the nation's largest organization that lobbies for honest, open, and accountable government. With its 38 state organizations, CC's goal is to maintain a citizen's lobby that oversees government and watches every move it makes.

CC has a long record of success at governmental reform. It led the enactment of the 26th amendment, lowering the voting age from 21 to 18 and bringing millions of young Americans into the voting process. It was instrumental in opening Congressional committee meetings to the public and forcing public votes on legislation.

Since its inception, CC has been in the forefront of campaign finance reform. Its efforts led to the first limits on contributions and disclosure requirements, and it played a strong role in passage of the Freedom of Information Act.

CC led the multi-year campaign to ban "soft money." ("Hard money" is contributed directly to a candidate or a political party; "soft money" is contributed to groups that engage in political activity. Soft money can be spent on issues but cannot be spent on anything that specifically promotes or disparages a candidate.) This led to the enactment of the Bipartisan Campaign Reform Act (also called the McCain-Feingold Act).

In 2007, CC played a lead role in passing the Honest Leadership and Open Government Act, the most significant congressional ethics reform since the 1970s and the Watergate era.

The Christian Science Monitor has stated the following about CC: *"Common Cause ... has been an uncommonly successful lobby ... in terms of the depth and breadth of its efforts—in the Congress and state legislatures—there probably has never been a reform movement so active and with such a record of accomplishment."*

CC is a nonprofit, nonpartisan organization which, because of it extensive lobbying activities, is not tax exempt. CCEF, the Common Cause Education Fund, is its affiliate and is a tax-exempt public charity.

CCEF uses funding approximately as follows: program expenses, 94 %, administrative expenses, 3%, fundraising expenses, 3%.
For further information on both organizations:
Website: www.commoncause.org
Address: 133 19th St. NW, 9th Flr., Washington,
DC 20036
Telephone: 202-833-1200
Email: giving@commoncause.org

PICK ONE
HOW TO PROMOTE GOOD
GOVERNMENT AND PROTECT
INDIVIDUAL RIGHTS — THE NATION

Public Citizen (PC)

Public Citizen was founded in 1971 as a national, nonprofit advocacy (lobbying) organization to represent citizens' interests in Congress and the executive and judicial branches of government. It has a history of fierce independence and considerable success in the fight for openness and accountability in government. PC has upheld the rights of consumers for a great many issues, including social and economic justice, individual safety, environmental protection, effective and affordable health care, fair trade policies, campaign finance reform, transparent governance, etc.

Democrat, Republican, and Independent leaders have lauded PC as one of the most effective advocacy organizations for consumers. Among its long string of achievements: In 1974 PC successfully lobbied Congress to override a presidential veto to make strong improvements to the Freedom of Information Act. In 1976 PC stopped the use of a toxic red dye in foods and the use of chloroform in cough medicines and toothpaste. In 1981 PC thwarted President Reagan's attempt to abolish the Clean Air Act. In 1983 PC stopped the administration's attempt to revoke auto safety standards (air bags). In 1987 PC won a landmark court order prohibiting banks from holding checks for excessive time periods. In 1989 PC forced Congress to halt its exorbitant, self-determined pay raise and to prohibit financial awards (honoraria) to legislators. In 1990 PC forced the Nuclear Regulatory Commission to require minimum training standards for nuclear reactor workers. In 1992 PC won a court order forcing the Occupational Safety and Hazard Commission (OSHA) to halt the exposure of workers to toxic cadmium. In 1994 PC played a key role in making home equity scams illegal. In 1998 PC forced publication of a national list of doctors disciplined for malpractice and other malfeasance. In 1999 PC played a key role in passing truck safety legislation which resulted in the creation of the Motor Carrier Safety Administration, and it led the coalition that forced Firestone to recall 6.5 million defective auto tires.

The list goes on and on and it is impressive.

Public Citizen (PC) is the lobbying segment of the organization. Because of its active lobbying, by law donations to PC are *not* tax deductible. Public Citizen Foundation (PCF), its educational affiliate, does not engage in lobbying. Donations to PCF *are* tax deductible.

PC uses funding approximately as follows: program expenses, 65%, administrative expenses, 24%, fundraising expenses, 11%.
PCF uses funding approximately as follows: program expenses, 85.5 %, administrative expenses, 9.5%, fundraising expenses, 5%.
For further information on both organizations:
Website: www.citizen.org
Address:1600 20th Street, NW, Washington,
     DC 20009
Telephone: 202-588-1000
Email: member@citizen.org

PICK ONE
HOW TO PROMOTE GOOD
GOVERNMENT AND PROTECT
INDIVIDUAL RIGHTS — THE NATION

Center for Responsive Politics (CRP)

Founded in 1983, CRP is the nation's leading research organization that tracks money in politics. CRP works primarily through its website, OpenSecrets.org, which provides an amazing amount of information such as who donates money in politics, who receives it, and personal financial disclosures of elected and appointed officials. Contributions and lobbying can be tracked in several ways, including by industry and interest group.

Website users can even track who in their own communities have made political contributions—to whom and how much.

Currently, CRP has expanded its website to include even more aspects of money in politics, such as tracking congressional travel and identifying "revolving doors," where previously elected and appointed officials use their political influence to secure high paying jobs.

CRP is nonpartisan, independent, and nonprofit. The purpose of all the information provided is to educate voters, to have them become more involved in the political process, and to create a more transparent and responsive government.

CRP has won numerous awards for its OpenSecrets website. The organization relies on a combination of donations from private individuals and from foundations; it does not accept contributions from businesses, trade associations, or labor unions.

Center for Responsive Politics (CRP), continued

CRP uses funding approximately as follows:
program expenses, 83%, administrative expenses,
10%, fundraising expenses, 7%.
For further information:
Website: www.opensecrets.org
Address: 1101 14th Street, NW, Suite 1030,
    Washington, DC 20005
Telephone: 202-857-0044
Fax: 202-857-7809
Email: info@crp.org

Pick One
How to Promote Good Government and Protect Individual Rights — The Nation

American Civil Liberties Union (ACLU)

The ACLU is one of the controversial nongovernmental organizations operating in the U.S. This is because the mission of the ACLU is to protect *all* of the individual rights guaranteed by the Constitution *to everyone*, whether or not the issues involved are popular or unpopular.

Our system of government is that the majority rules through elected representatives but that the power of that rule is limited by the Bill of Rights and later amendments to the Constitution that protect individual rights. ACLU is dedicated to protecting: Our freedom of speech, association, and assembly. Our freedom of the press. Our freedom of religion. Our right to equal protection under the law, regardless of gender, race, or national origin. Our right to fair legal process. Our right not to have unwarranted government intrusion in our lives.

ACLU often focuses on groups that have traditionally been denied their rights, such as the poor, disabled people, gays and lesbians, racial and ethnic minorities, mental health patients, prisoners, etc.

Sometimes ACLU has to stand firm on its principles in the face of powerful opposition, as when it has defended the rights of abhorrent groups such as neo-nazis or the Ku Klux Klan. The organization has paid dearly for these controversial stands in terms of its popularity and financial support, but ACLU maintains that the government cannot decide what we are allowed to see and hear; each individual gets to decide that, and if the rights of unpopular or vulnerable groups are denied, all of our rights are threatened.

ACLU has grown to more than 500,000 members and supporters. The organization maintains affiliates in every state and in Puerto Rico, and it annually defends some 6000 court cases where individual rights have been denied. The local affiliates lobby state legislatures, host public forums, and provide legal assistance.

ACLU is divided into two separate entities for tax purposes. The ACLU primarily does legislative lobbying while the ACLU Foundation provides legal presentation in cases involving civil rights and it has an outreach program to educate the public on these rights. Contributions to the ACLU Foundation are tax-deductible while those to ACLU are not.

While the ACLU is often controversial, many liberals and conservatives, government and non-government leaders, and academic and business leaders have praised ACLU as the vanguard of individual rights in America.

> ACLU uses funding approximately as follows: program expenses, 80%, administrative expenses, 11%, fundraising expenses, 9%.
> For further information:
> Website: www.aclu.org
> Address: 125 Broad St., 18th Flr., New York, NY 10004
> Telephone: 212-549-2573
> Email: fdngift@aclu.org

PICK ONE
HOW TO PROMOTE GOOD
GOVERNMENT AND PROTECT
INDIVIDUAL RIGHTS — THE NATION

National Legal Aid and Defender Association (NLADA)

It has now been more than forty years since the Supreme Court declared that everyone has a right to legal counsel when they face incarceration due to criminal charges. *Yet every day in this country people are convicted in courtrooms without ever seeing a lawyer.*

In 1974 Congress created and funded the Legal Services Corporation to assure legal assistance to those unable to afford it. *Yet most individuals who are eligible to receive this mandated legal assistance still do not get it.*

NLADA is the oldest, largest, and arguably the most effective advocate for fairness in the justice system for low-income and indigent clients. It advocates for individuals who are convicted not because they have committed a crime but because they are poor. It advocates for children who are abused in group homes and shelters because of inadequate legal help. It advocates for those who are not allowed to die with dignity because they do not have the legal aid to obtain proper medical treatment.

NLADA's members are civil lawyers, criminal defenders, legal scholars, community activists, and large numbers of the lay public. Together they represent the largest and most powerful ambassadors for equal justice in the nation.

The goal of NLADA is to end the travesties in our courtrooms that occur because people have a lack of resources, because of their race, because they do not speak good English, or because they simply do not understand the charges against them. And it means to do this by helping to create well-funded legal aid and public defender systems that really do deliver competent services in every state and territory of the U.S.

National Legal Aid and Defender Association
(NLADA), continued

NLADA uses funding approximately as follows:
program expenses, 81%, administrative expenses, 7%,
fundraising expenses, 12%.
For further information:
Website: www.nlada.org
Address: 1140 Connecticut Ave., #900, Washington,
    DC 20036
Telephone: 202-452-0620
Fax: 202-872-1031
Email: info@nlada.org

PICK ONE
HOW TO PROMOTE TRADITIONAL
VALUES OR END DISCRIMINATION
THE NATION

American Family Association (AFA)

Don Wildmon, an ordained United Methodist minister, founded the National Federation for Decency in 1977. The organization became the American Family Association in 1988.

AFA stands for traditional family values and focuses primarily on the negative influence of television and other media on society. The organization claims the entertainment industry has played the major role in the decline of values upon which our country was founded, and that it is essential to hold responsible the companies that sponsor programs that attack those values. It also believes it is important to commend those companies that support programs whose influence is positive.

AFA seeks to motivate citizens to change the current culture to reflect scriptural truth. It fights against the normalization of premarital sex, and has led the fight to influence television sponsors to end pro-homosexual programming. It has distributed some 400,000 copies of the *Fight Back Book*, a resource guide to television advertisers.

AFA has an active anti-pornography campaign and has led the fight to eliminate funding for programs of the National Endowment of the Arts with which it disagrees.

Organization members receive a monthly letter addressing specific issues of concern and recommendations for taking action.

American Family Association (AFA), continued

AFA uses funding approximately as follows:
program expenses, 91.5%, administrative expenses,
4.5%, fundraising expense, 4%
For further information:
Website: www.afa.net
Address: P.O. Drawer 2440, Tupelo, MS 38803
Telephone: 662- 844-5036
Fax: 662-842-7798
Email: foundation@afa.net

PICK ONE
HOW TO PROMOTE TRADITIONAL VALUES OR END DISCRIMINATION
THE NATION

Lambda Legal (LL)

LL is a national organization that promotes the rights and full equality of gays, lesbians, bisexuals, transgenders (known as LGBT people), and those with HIV. The organization pursues litigation, is an advocate for legislation, and has a public outreach program to educate the public. The goal is to have the highest possible impact on laws, policies, and attitudes.

From its national headquarters in New York and from its regional offices, LL's legal experts select cases that will have the greatest effect of ensuring the rights LGBT and HIV people. This work involves a variety of issues, including equality on the job, relationship and parenting rights, protection against discrimination because of sexual orientation, gender identity, or HIV status.

LL maintains a national network of legal volunteers that enables interested lawyers, legal assistants, and law students to become involved and work with the LL staff.

Legal cases are augmented by highly publicized public education campaigns across the country.

LL believes that its work benefits everyone, for when discrimination is eliminated or mostly reduced, the nation becomes a better place for its tolerance.

Lambda Legal (LL), continued

LL uses funding approximately as follows: program
expenses, 71%, administrative expenses, 11%,
fundraising expenses, 18%.
For further information:
Website: www.lambdalegal.org
Address: 120 Wall St., Ste. 1500, New York, NY 10005
Telephone: 212-809-8585
Fax: 212- 809-0055
Email: members@lambdalegal.org

Pick One
How to Promote Gun Rights
or Gun Limits — The Nation

Brady Center To Prevent Gun Violence (BCPGV)

The goal of BCPGV is to create a nation where all citizens are safe from gun violence at home, at work, at school, and everywhere in their communities. It works to enact legislation and to enforce sensible regulations to reduce gun violence. BCPGV is the nation's largest, non-partisan, grassroots organization leading the fight to prevent gun violence.

Its several programs include Law Enforcement Relations, The Legal Action Project, God Not Guns Coalition, Hispanic/Latino Outreach, African-American Outreach, Linking with Victims for Change Network, Steps to Prevent Firearm Injury in the Home, and the Million Mom March chapters.

BCPGV seeks to improve public policies by strong grassroots activism, a public education program and election of public officials who support gun laws. A priority of the organization is to enact reasonable regulations of the gun industry.

A goal of the organization is to significantly reduce the flow of arms by licensed, unethical gun dealers through their program, the Campaign Against Illegal Guns.

BCPGV is working to extend background checks *for all gun sales*. It is working to renew the Assault Weapons Ban. It is trying to get legislation enacted to tighten safety standards for all guns.

BCPGV is not an anti-gun organization. It believes that law-abiding citizens should be able to keep firearms. But the group also insists upon sensible gun laws to keep guns out of the hands of those who should not have them; that certain kinds of weapons should not be allowed for private ownership; and that gun owners should be well trained in the highest safety standards.

Poll after poll confirms that the majority of Americans support sensible gun laws. And while BCPGV realizes that it will continue to be vastly outspent by the powerful pro-gun lobbies, the ultimate trend is to life-saving laws to reduce gun violence in America.

As a lobbying organization, donations are not tax-deductible.

BCPGV uses funding approximately as follows: Program expenses, 77.5%, administrative expenses, 6.5%, fundraising expenses, 16%.
For further information:
Website: www.bradycenter.org
Address: 1225 Eye Street NW, Ste.1100,
    Washington, DC 20005
Telephone: 202-289-7319
Fax: 202-408-1851
Email: info@bradycenter.org

PICK ONE
HOW TO PROMOTE GUN RIGHTS
OR GUN LIMITS — THE NATION

Gun Owners of America (GOA)

Founded in 1975, GOA is a nonprofit lobbying organization dedicated to preserving the 2nd Amendment rights of gun owners. The organization believes that Americans have lost gun rights over the years and works to bring them back. GOA is proud of the fact that among pro-gun organizations it is considered the "no compromise" gun lobby.

GOA has put together a legal network to help protect gun owner's rights in almost every state in the nation. The organization's staff works with members of Congress, state legislators and local officials to fight against closures of gun clubs and gun ranges by overzealous government agencies. One example of GOA's success was fighting for and winning the court battle over the right of gun owners to sue and recover damages from the Bureau of Alcohol, Tobacco and Firearms (BATF) for harassment and unlawful seizure of firearms.

Recently, new software has been created to educate gun dealers to avoid technicalities that permit the BATF to cancel their licenses. According to GOA, BATF has been trying to suppress this software, and GOA is fighting to ensure its availability.

As stated by the organization, "From state legislatures and city councils to the United States Congress and the White House, GOA represents the views of gun owners whenever their rights are threatened. GOA has never wavered from its mission to defend the Second Amendment—liberty's freedom teeth, as George Washington called it."

As a lobbying organization, donations to GOA are not tax deductible.

Gun Owners of America (GOA), continued

GOA uses funding approximately as follows:
program expenses, 71%, administrative expenses,
13%, fundraising expenses, 16%.
For further information:
Website: www.gunowners.org
Address: 8001 Forbes Place, Ste.102, Springfield,
 VA 22151
Telephone: 703-321-8585
Fax: 703-321-8408

PICK ONE
HOW TO PROMOTE GUN RIGHTS
OR GUN LIMITS — THE NATION

Violence Policy Center (VPC)

According to VPC, "Each year, more than 30,000 Americans die in gun suicides, homicides, and unintentional shootings as a result of the ready availability, and accessibility, of specific classes of firearms. Gun violence is more than a crime issue; it is a broad-based public health crisis of which crime is merely the most recognized aspect."

VPC is dedicated to stopping this annual toll of injury and death through its research and educational programs. Rather than the traditional freedom vs. violence battles, VPC sees gun violence as a public health issue that should be subject to the same health and safety standards that apply to all consumer products. The organization states that guns and tobacco are the only two consumer products for which there is no federal health and safety oversight. This approach to gun violence as a health issue has already been enacted in California and Massachusetts.

VPC is known as the most aggressive and effective gun control organization in the U.S. It has a record of successes including ending the loophole of improper sales at gun shows, reducing the number of gun dealers (from 250,000 to less than 55,000), banning the possession of weapons by domestic violence offenders, and revealing how the gun industry markets to women and children. VPC exposed and helped end the federally funded program that allowed thousands of convicted felons to own guns—at taxpayers' expense! With its publication of *Making A Killing*, VPC revealed how the firearms industry has increased lethality of its products in an attempt to increase gun sales.

Each year VPC publishes a number of high-impact, fact-based studies on gun violence issues. VPC is frequently used as a reliable information source by the media and policymakers, and the organization works with a large number of other national, state and local groups to keep homes, schools, workplaces and neighborhoods safe from gun violence.

Donations to VPC are tax-deductible.

VPC uses funding approximately as follows: program expenses, 88%, administrative expenses, 9.5%, fundraising expenses, 2.5%.
For further information:
Website: www.vpc.org
Address: 1730 Rhode Island Avenue NW, Ste. 1014, Washington, DC 20036
Telephone: 202-822 8200

PICK ONE
HOW TO PROMOTE GUN RIGHTS
OR GUN LIMITS — THE NATION

National Rifle Association (NRA)

With its nearly four million members, the NRA is widely accepted as America's foremost defender of 2nd Amendment rights and as the leader in firearms education all over the world.

NRA has a large number of programs of all kinds, including competition shooting matches, shooting range services, hunter's services, gunsmith schools, a national firearms museum, women's programs, and youth programs and scholarships.

With its NRA Police Firearms Instructor certification program, NRA is the only national trainer of law enforcement officers. There are now some 10,000 NRA-certified police and security firearms instructors.

For civilian training, NRA is the undisputed leader in firearms education. There are now some 55,000 NRA-certified instructors who train about 750,000 gun owners each year. And the NRA's child safety program ("Stop. Don't touch. Leave the area. Tell an adult.") has been seen by more than 21 million children from kindergarten to 6th grade.

In 1990 the NRA established the NRA Foundation (NRAF) which ensures the financial support for firearms-related activities such as funding gun safety and other educational programs of benefit to the general public. Donations to the NRAF are tax-deductible while donations to the NRA are not.

National Rifle Association (NRA), continued

NRA uses funding approximately as follows:
program expenses, 72%, administrative expenses,
15%, fundraising expenses, 13%.
For further information:
NRA Website: www.nrahq.org
Address: 11250 Waples Mill Rd., Fairfax, VA 22030
Telephone: 800-672-3888
NRAF telephone: 800-423-6894
NRAF email: nraf@nrahq.org

SELECTED SPECIALIZED CHARITIES

PICK ONE
SELECTED SPECIALIZED CHARITIES
(in alphabetical order)

Americans for Nonsmokers' Rights (ANR)

ANR is a recognized leader in the promotion of nonsmokers' rights in the U.S. and other countries around the world. Its main goals are to educate the community about the health effects of secondhand smoke and the benefits of smoke-free environments, and to help raise a smoke-free generation.

Founded in 1976, ANR began by lobbying legislators and other policymakers to protect nonsmokers in the workplace and in enclosed public spaces. By assisting countries, legislative districts, and communities, ANR has taken on the tobacco industry and helped thousands of municipalities to pass smoke-free regulations. Due in part to ANR's work, 16 countries now have 100% smoke-free regulations in workplaces, restaurants, or bars.

ANR members receive Action Alerts on smokers' rights issues and the organization provides assistance to local groups that are trying to enact, implement or protect smoke-free laws, including the dissemination of model ordinances.

The ANR Foundation (ANRF) is the organization's non-lobbying, public education arm. ANRF supports the efforts of ANR and provides education materials for schools, public health departments, and medical facilities.

Americans for Nonsmokers' Rights (ANR), continued

ANRF uses funding approximately as follows:
program expenses, 87%, administrative expenses,
10%, fundraising expenses, 3%.
For further information:
Website: www.no-smoke.org
Address: 2530 San Pablo Avenue, Suite J, Berkeley,
    CA 94702
Telephone: 510-841-3032
Fax: 510-841-3071
Email: anr@no-smoke.org

PICK ONE
SELECTED SPECIALIZED CHARITIES
(in alphabetical order)

Arbor Day Foundation (ADF)

Founded in 1972, ADF is the world's oldest and largest tree-planting organization. Their mission envisions a world where trees and forests are abundant, healthy, and sustainable, and highly valued by all people. Each year more than eight million trees are distributed to ADF members, and over 700,000 trees are planted in America's national forests. Since ADF activities are both in the U.S. and worldwide, this organization is listed here and in the Nation category.

ADF operates several different programs, including Rain Forest Rescue (for every $10 donation, 2500 square feet of rain forest is saved in the name of the donor), Tree City USA (which encourages cities to plant trees and provides the standards and information to sustain them), Nature Explore Club (helps educators, caregivers, and parents connect young children with nature), and Arbor Day Farm (which serves as an educational facility for foresters, environmentalists, etc).

ADF is supported by donations, selling trees and merchandise, and by several corporate sponsors.

ADF uses funding as follows: program expenses, 89%, administrative expenses, 2%, fundraising expenses, 9%.
For further information:
Website: www.arborday.org
Address: 211 North 12th St., Lincoln, NE 68508
Telephone: 402-474-5655

Pick One
Selected Specialized Charities
(in alphabetical order)

Ducks Unlimited (DU)

DU is not only the world's largest conservation organization dedicated specifically to waterfowl and wetlands, it is one of the largest conservation groups in the world with more than one million supporters in the U.S. Canada, Mexico, Australia, New Zealand, and Europe.

Founded in 1937, DU has been able to protect more than nine million acres of nesting, brood-rearing, migration, and wintering habitat throughout North America. As part of its conservation efforts, DU's work improves flood control and water quality in wetlands, and creates new recreational opportunities.

Some 90% of the organization's members are hunters. The organization's vision is to protect and restore enough wetlands to fill the skies with waterfowl and to value and enjoy the sport of hunting. DU provides many services to waterfowl hunters, including migration maps, hunting area advisories, waterfowl identification and species habits, hunting tips, and retriever training.

While the loss and degradation of wetlands and adjacent nesting cover due to development, pollution, and drought continues to have a negative impact, with the help of DU most populations of geese have increased; and all but a few species of prairie-nesting ducks have made recoveries.

It is only with strong support from its members that DU will be able to meet the challenge to restore quality habitat in all the key waterfowl areas of North America.

Ducks Unlimited (DU), continued

> DU uses funding approximately as follows:
> program expenses, 82.5%, administrative expenses,
> 2.5%, fundraising expenses, 15%.
> For further information:
> Website: www.ducks.org
> Address: 1 Waterfowl Way, Memphis, TN 38120
> Telephone: 800-453-8257
> Email: jrich@ducks.org

PICK ONE
SELECTED SPECIALIZED CHARITIES

(in alphabetical order)

Endangered Language Fund (ELF)

ELF was founded ten years ago with the goal of supporting endangered language preservation and documentation projects. Their mechanism for supporting this effort is by modest grants to individuals, tribes, and museums. Although a very small organization, ELF has issued 97 grants for work in more than 30 countries. These grants range from the development of radio programs in Native American indigenous languages in South Dakota to recording the last living oral historian of the Shor language of Western Siberia.

Each year ELF receives a large number of grant proposals for work on endangered languages around the world—only a few of which they can afford to fund.

ELF is also developing an outreach program designed to teach students about the present diversity of languages, why so many are disappearing, and the reasons for preserving or at least documenting them before they are gone. An aspect of this educational program is for students to explore why some languages are spoken by millions of people while others decline or disappear completely.

ELF has a very modest donations and expenses base. There is no paid staff and it uses donations almost exclusively for grants to others for work on languages.

For further information:
Website: www.endangeredlanguagefund.org
Address: 300 George Street, Suite 900, New Haven, CT 06511
Telephone: 203-865-6163, ext. 265
Fax: 203-865-8963
Email: elf@endangeredlanguagefund.org

Pick One
Selected Specialized Charities
(in alphabetical order)

National Public Radio (NPR)

NPR is a privately supported, not-for-profit, membership organization with an audience of some 26 million listeners. NPR isn't a government agency, it isn't a radio station, and it doesn't own any stations; what it does is produce original radio programs and distributes them to more than 860 independently operated, noncommercial public radio stations. Each NPR member station serves its audience with a combination of NPR's programming and its choice of its own local programming.

The organization produces more than 130 hours of original programming each week, including news magazines All Things Considered®. and Morning Edition®, a variety of music, interview and information programming, plus breaking news stories.

Each NPR station designs its own broadcasting by combining these NPR-produced programs with its own local programming. NPR also distributes programs internationally via NPR Worldwide.

A great many listeners depend on NPR programs and the organization has won countless awards for its many programs in the public interest.

NPR receives most of its funding from local, public radio stations. You can help by supporting any of the 860 local stations. A local station search is available on the NPR website.

National Public Radio (NPR), continued

NPR uses funding approximately as follows: program expenses, 78.5%, administrative expenses, 18%, fundraising expenses, 3.5%. It receives most of its funding from local, public radio stations.
For further information:
Website: www.npr.org
Address: 635 Massachusetts Avenue, NW,
    Washington, DC 20001
Telephone: 202-513-2000
Fax: 202-513-3329
Email: asporkin@npr.org

Pick One
Selected Specialized Charities

(in alphabetical order)

ProEnglish (PE)

PE is the largest national, nonprofit organization whose goal is to protect English as the common language of the U.S. The organization believes that while the individual right to speak foreign languages must be respected, government should promote the one language that unites us rather than institutionalize the different languages that divide us. Therefore, PE seeks to influence policymakers to adopt laws or constitutional amendments declaring English the official language of the U.S. and of the individual states.

PE seeks to repeal current federal mandates that require government documents and voting ballots to be translated into languages other than English.

While our nation's public schools have the clear responsibility to help foreign-speaking students learn English, PE seeks to end prolonged bilingual education where students have classes in their native language and are not subject to immersion in English.

All candidates for U.S. citizenship should be required to demonstrate their ability to use English and to understand our system of government. Naturalization ceremonies should only be conducted in English.

Public agencies and private businesses and other institutions must often deal with legal challenges concerning language. With its expertise in the field of language law, PE provides free legal assistance to these entities that face litigation or regulatory actions over language.

ProEnglish (PE), continued

PE uses funding approximately as follows:
program expenses, 83%, administrative expenses, 9%,
fundraising expenses, 8%.
For further information:
Website: www.proenglish.org
Address: 1601 N Kent St., Ste. 1100, Arlington,
    VA 22209
Telephone: 703-816-8821
Fax: 703-816-8824
Email: mail@proenglish.org

PICK ONE
SELECTED SPECIALIZED CHARITIES
(in alphabetical order)

Special Olympics (SO)

Special Olympics was founded with the idea of helping to bring all persons with intellectual disabilities into the larger society under conditions whereby they are accepted, respected, and given a chance to become productive citizens. It is a tenet of SO that people with intellectual disabilities can benefit from and enjoy participation in individual and team sports, and that the most appropriate venue is when the participation is among those of equal abilities.

All SO activities reflect the values, standards, traditions, ceremonies, and events embodied in the modern Olympic movement, modified to better enhance the dignity and self-esteem of the participants.

Everyone with an intellectual disability who is at least eight years old is eligible to participate, regardless of their degree of disability or economic circumstance. Year-round sports training is available from qualified coaches, and sports activities are designed to complement the age and ability level of each participant.

SO is run by some 700,000 volunteers worldwide. Involvement can be anything from a one-day scorekeeper at an athletic event to year-round at several hours per week. Volunteers can be active at their local community programs, or at the state, national, and international levels. Volunteers include civic and fraternal groups, high school and college students, amateur and professional athletes, coaches, teachers, parents, retirees, corporate employees, etc.

Volunteers often report that their experiences with SO have been among the most rewarding of their lives. To find the nearest Special Olympics chapter near you, use the Program Locator on the SO website.

Special Olympics (SO), continued

SO uses funding approximately as follows: program expenses, 81%, administrative expenses, 4.5%, fundraising expenses, 14.5%.
For further information:
Website: www.specialolympics.org
National HQ Address: 1133 19th Street, N.W.,
    Washington, DC 20036
Telephone: 202-628-3630
Fax: 202-824-0200
Email: info@specialolympics.org

PICK ONE
SELECTED SPECIALIZED CHARITIES
(in alphabetical order)

The Tibet Fund (TF)

Among several funds to aid Tibetans, this is the one founded by the Dalai Lama in 1981. Its purpose is to sustain the Tibetan way of life by helping the 140,000 refugees that make up the Tibetan exile communities in India, Nepal and Bhutan, and in Tibetan communities in several other countries of the world, including the U.S.

TF also supports programs inside Tibet that are lacking, especially in the areas of health, education, and small business development. A serious problem in Tibet is cataract blindness, and TF has constructed an eye care hospital and sponsors traveling eye camps which are able to provide on-site corrective surgery. The organization supports many orphanages throughout Tibet. And there are the English Language and Computer Training Programs that are located both in Tibet and in several locations in China where there are large Tibetan populations. TF also supports an exchange program that brings Tibetan students at the college level to study in America.

The Tibetan people realize and appreciate that they are supported by benevolent people throughout the world. The Dalai Lama has often said that were it not for the generosity of individuals, organizations, and governments in the world community, the culture, religion, and identity of the Tibetan people would have been effectively eliminated.

The Tibetan people want to do more than attract sympathy, however. They want to set an example of free people that can create democratic institutions based on compassion, non-violence and justice, and self-help and self-determination.

The Tibet Fund (TF), continued

TF uses funding approximately as follows:
program expenses, 93.5%, administrative expenses,
5%, fundraising expenses, 1.5%
For further information:
Website: www.tibetfund.org
Address: 241 East 32nd St., New York, NY 10016
Telephone: 212-213-5011
Fax: 212-213-1219
Email: info@tibetfund.org

PICK ONE
SELECTED SPECIALIZED CHARITIES
(in alphabetical order)

Trout Unlimited (TU)

Founded in 1959, TU's mission is to "…conserve, protect, and restore North America's coldwater fisheries and their watersheds." To accomplish this, TU maintains a staff of conservation experts, policy advocates, and lawyers, and the organization has more than 150,000 volunteers who operate across the U.S. in 450 chapters.

Since its inception, TU has operated on the basis of employing the best science. TU's first president, Dr. Casey Westell Jr., stated, "In all matters of trout management, we want to know that we are substantially correct, both morally and biologically." To this end the organization has developed a series of unique tools to evaluate fish populations, including the Conservation Success Index for evaluating the health of coldwater species.

TU collaborates with several other conservation groups, local communities, and state and federal agencies to rebuild the health and resiliency of watersheds.

In the coming years, TU is working to ensure that populations of coldwater fish are restored in sufficient numbers so that healthy fisheries will once again thrive across North America.

TU uses funding approximately as follows: program expenses, 82.5%, administrative expenses, 5%, fundraising expenses, 12.5%.
For further information:
Website: www.tu.org
Address: 1300 N. 17th St., #500, Arlington, VA 22209
Telephone: 800-834-2419
Fax: 703-284-9400
Email: membership@tu.org

Pick One
Selected Specialized Charities

(in alphabetical order)

WaterAid America (WAA)

WAA is one of the leading independent nonprofit organizations dedicated to providing the world's poorest people with access to safe water, sanitation, and hygiene education. The organization has offices and working groups in 17 African, Asian, and Pacific countries.

WAA works with local communities to help them set up and maintain water and sanitation systems that are in accordance with local needs and abilities. In developing countries, local government agencies are often given the responsibility to develop water and sanitation systems, but they frequently lack the skills and resources to accomplish this. WAA works closely with local workers to develop their skills to enable them to fulfill the responsibilities given them.

The organization believes that these three services-providing safe water and effective sanitation, plus teaching good hygiene practices are prerequisites for all other development, including improving livelihoods, education, and health care.

WAA has an outreach program to educate the developed world as to why water and sanitation are vital to reducing poverty. To this end, WAA is committed to helping half the proportion of people living in poverty around the world by 2015 (the UN Millennium Development Goal).

Although WAA works primarily on long-term solutions, it also responds to natural disasters and other emergencies in testing for water safety and protecting and restoring damaged water and sanitation systems.

To accomplish its work, WAA has partnered with organizations and institutions such as World Wildlife Fund, Columbia University, Natural Resources Defense Council, Oxfam, UCLA, Asia Society,

London School of Hygiene and Tropical Medicine, and Church World Service.

> WAA uses funding approximately as follows: Program expenses, 84%, administrative expenses, 10%, fundraising expenses, 6%.
> For further information:
> Website: www.wateraid.org
> Address: 232 Madison Ave., New York, NY 10016
> Telephone: 212-683-0430
> Fax: 212-683-0293
> Email: email contact is on website

CHARITIES
LISTING
FOR
MEDICAL
SPECIALTIES

PICK ONE
MEDICAL SPECIALTIES

Here is a selection of the major charities for specific diseases that have received high ratings from the major charity rating organizations, followed by their websites.

AIDS
Elton John Aids Foundation – www.ejaf.org
National Aids Fund – www.aidsfund.org
Elizabeth Glazer Pediatric Aids Foundation – www.pedaids.org
American Foundation for Aids Research – www.amfar.org

ALZHEIMER'S
Alzheimer's Association – www.alz.org

ALS
Amyotrophic Lateral Sclerosis Association – www.alsa.org

ASTHMA and LUNG DISEASE
American Lung Association – www.lungusa.org

AUTISM
Autism Society of America – www.autism-society.org

BIRTH DEFECTS
Kennedy Krieger Research Institute – www.kennedykrieger.org

BLINDNESS
Prevent Blindness America – www.preventblindness.org

BRAIN and SPINAL CORD DISORDERS
American Brain Tumor Association – www.abta.org
Brain Tumor Society – www.braintumor.org

CANCER
Cancer Care – www.cancercare.org
Cancer Research and Prevention Foundation –
   www.ppreventcancer.org
Cancer Research Institute – www.cancerresearch.org
Cancer Treatment Research Foundation –
   www.gatewayforcancerresearch.org
National Breast Cancer Coalition Fund – www.stopbreastcancer.org
Prostate Cancer Foundation – www.prostatecancerfoundation.org
Skin Cancer Foundation – www.skincancer.org
Susan G. Komen Breast Cancer Foundation – www.koman.org

CYSTIC FIBROSIS
Cystic Fibrosis Foundation – www.cff.org
Cystic Fibrosis Research, Inc. – www.cfri.org

DIABETES
Juvenile Diabetes Research Foundation – www.jdrf.org
Sansum Diabetes Research Institute – www.sansum.org

DOWN SYNDROME
National Down Syndrome Society – www.ndss.org

EPILEPSY
Epilepsy Foundation – www.epilepsyfoundation.org

HEART DISEASE
American Heart Association – www.americanheart.org

HEMOPHILIA
National Hemophilia Foundation – www.hemophilia.org

HUNTINGTON'S DISEASE
Huntington's Disease Society of America – www.hdsa.org

KIDNEY DISEASE
American Kidney Fund – www.kidneyfund.org
National Kidney Foundation – www.kidney.org

LEUKEMIA and LYMPHOMA
Leukemia and Lymphoma Society – www.leukemia-lymphoma.org
Lymphoma Research Foundation – www.lymphoma.org

LIVER DISEASE
Hepatitis B Foundation – www.hepb.org

LUPUS
Lupus Foundation of America – www.lupus.org

MENTAL DISORDERS
National Alliance on Mental Illness – www.nami.org

MULTIPLE SCLEROSIS
National Multiple Sclerosis Society – www.nationalmssociety.org

MUSCULAR DYSTROPHY
Muscular Dystrophy Association – www.mda.org

PARKINSON'S DISEASE
American Parkinson Disease Association – www.apdaparkinson.org
Parkinson's Action Network – www.parkinsonsaction.org

REPRODUCTIVE HEALTH
Center for Reproductive Rights – www.reproductiverights.org
La Leche League International – www.llli.org
National Campaign to Prevent Teen Pregnancy –
    www.thenationalcampaign.org
Planned Parenthood Federation of America –
    www.plannedparenthood.org

SICKLE CELL DISASE

Sickle Cell Disease Association of America –
www. sicklecelldisease.org

SKIN DISEASE

Skin Cancer Foundation – www.skincancer.org

SPINA BIFIDA

Spina Bifida Association of America – www.sbaa.org

STROKE

National Stroke Association – www.stroke.org

SUDDEN INFANT DEATH SYNDROME

Sudden Infant Death Syndrome Alliance – www.sids.org

TRANSPLANTS

Childrens Organ Transplant Association – www.cota.org
Mid-America Transplant Services – www.mts-stl.org
National Foundation for Transplants – www.transplants.org

WAYS TO VOLUNTEER

PICK ONE
WAYS TO VOLUNTEER

Since the early days of its beginning, the United States has been a nation of citizens who volunteer their services. That ethic remains strong today as people of all ages and abilities volunteer their time, skills, and energy to improve their communities. Volunteers mentor students, clean up after disasters, coach sports teams, donate skilled trade and professional services, help at hospitals, beautify parks, help the disabled, provide rides, gather food and clothing for the needy as well as a host of other things.

Volunteering has been, and continues to be, a necessary part of what constitutes life in America. There are literally thousands of nonprofit organizations that could not exist without volunteers. In the other sections of this book you'll find specific charitable organizations that focus on diverse needs. Essentially all of these organizations need and actively recruit volunteers, and many of them also have internship programs.

The U.S. government has strongly encouraged volunteering. In 1993 the Corporation for National and Community Service (CNCS) was established by legislation to help connect people with opportunities to help their communities and the nation. The creation of CNCS merged several volunteer agencies, including the Senior Corps, Americorps, VISTA, and Learn and Serve America under a single umbrella. You can find much valuable information on the CNCS website, whose address is www.nationalservice.org. If you are interested in data on volunteering throughout the nation, including cities and regions, CNCS also provides a wealth of information on its sister website, www.volunteeringinamerica.gov.

To help locate services in your own community that need volunteers, try your local chamber of commerce or the visitor's center. Many communities also have ministerial associations that coordinate the charitable activities of local churches. And many county governments publish a list of resources that need volunteers, such as a seniors resource guide.

In addition, almost all nonprofit organizations, including those listed in this book, utilize volunteers; some at their central locations and others in widely scattered field facilities. Contact them directly for more information.

Included in the list that follows are also additional resources whose sole purpose is to connect volunteers with opportunities.

Here are several organizations that need *and make good use* of volunteers.

Pick One
Ways to Volunteer

(in alphabetical order)

AFS-USA (formerly American Field Service)

The student and teacher exchange programs of AFS are made possible by granting institutions, support of the U.S. State Department, individual donations, and by some 37,000 volunteers all over the world. Volunteers include men and women, young and old, professionals, retirees, teachers and students, etc.

AFS volunteers help by locating and interviewing students and families for potential exchanges, serving as a contact person for a student or teacher from another country, arranging AFS group activities for students, and so on.

In addition to the satisfaction of helping others, AFS volunteers gain experience in inter-cultural communication and develop language and leadership skills. AFS also provides training of volunteers for leadership roles at the local, national, and international levels.

The majority of volunteers are themselves former AFS students and teachers who have found the exchange program so satisfying and a real agent for helping to create a more peaceful world that they continue to volunteer years after their initial involvement.

For further information:
Website: www.afs.org/usa
Address: 71 West 23rd Street, 17th Floor, New York
    NY 10010-4102
Telephone: 212-299-9000
Fax: 212-807-1001
Email: afsinfo@afs.org

Pick One
Ways to Volunteer
(in alphabetical order)

American Red Cross (ARC)

Approximately 1.2 million people volunteer for the ARC, and volunteers make up 97% of all ARC staff. Volunteers come from all walks of life, and over 40% of volunteers are people under the age of 25.

Every year the ARC responds to more than 70,000 disasters. To assist in this, about 11 million volunteers have learned first aid, CPR, swimming and other health and safety skills.

Half the nation's blood supply—six million pints annually—is collected by more than 155,000 Red Cross volunteers. Others help deliver urgent messages for members of the armed forces as well as reconnecting thousands of families separated by conflicts and natural disasters. From drivers for the elderly escort program, to courses on HIV/AIDS care, to youth group coordinators, to local disaster responders, to classes on safe baby-sitting, there are literally hundreds of different areas where the ARC needs volunteers.

Whether you work with children, want safety training for employees, are a professional rescuer, or simply want to know how to help someone in an emergency, the American Red Cross has programs for volunteers.

> For further general information:
> Website: www.redcross.org
> Address: 2025 E Street NW, Washington, DC 20006
> Telephone: 202-303-4498
> For information on volunteering in your area:
> Website: www.redcross.volunteermatch.org

PICK ONE
WAYS TO VOLUNTEER
(in alphabetical order)

Blood Banks (Donating Blood and/or Volunteering)

There is a constant need for donated blood by persons with certain illnesses, those undergoing surgeries, accident victims, etc. Blood is something money can't buy—it is a gift from one person to another. And one donation of blood can save up to three lives.

To donate blood you must be at least 17 years old, weigh at least 110 lbs., and be in good health. The whole procedure of donating blood takes about one hour. After a slight pinch, the process is painless. Needles and collection bags are used only once and then discarded, so the donor can't be infected. After the procedure, snacks and drinks are offered. Donating blood does not cause tiredness or weakness.

Currently there are shortages of donated blood all across the country. If only one percent more of Americans would give blood, all of the shortages would be eliminated.

Volunteers are crucial to the operation of blood banks. Volunteer activities include greeters who explain procedures to first-time donors and reassure them, couriers, language translators, canteen operators, and those whose sole duty is to make sure donors are comfortable. Blood banks want to ensure that first-time donors have a good experience so they become regular donors.

Listed below are some of the largest blood banks in the U.S. Look at their websites to find blood banks in or near your community.

> For further information:
> American Association of Blood Banks (AABB),
>   website: www.aabb.org
> American Red Cross, website: www.givelife.org
> America's Blood Centers, website.
>   www.americasblood.org

Pick One
Ways to Volunteer

(in alphabetical order)

Ducks Unlimited (DU)

DU is not only the world's largest conservation organization dedicated specifically to waterfowl and wetlands, it is one of the largest conservation groups in the world with more than one million supporters in the U.S. Canada, Mexico, Australia, New Zealand, and Europe.

Founded in 1937, DU has been able to protect more than nine million acres of nesting, brood-rearing, migration, and wintering habitat throughout North America. As part of its conservation efforts, DU's work improves flood control and water quality in wetlands, and creates new recreational opportunities.

Some 90% of the organization's members are hunters. The organization's vision is to protect and restore enough wetlands to fill the skies with waterfowl and to value and enjoy the sport of hunting. DU provides many services to waterfowl hunters, including migration maps, hunting area advisories, waterfowl identification and species habits, hunting tips, and retriever training.

Volunteers pay an essential role in the work of DU. To become involved with DU's conservation work, see the website to find your nearest chapter. An excellent way to play a significant roll is to become a DU conservation intern.

Other volunteers run local, state and national events, help with fundraising and coordinate with businesses that underwrite DU events and conservation efforts.

While the loss and degradation of wetlands and adjacent nesting cover due to development, pollution and drought continues to have a negative impact, with the help of DU most populations of geese have increased and all but a few species of prairie-nesting ducks have made recoveries.

It is only with strong support from its volunteers that DU will be able to meet the challenge to restore quality habitat in all the key waterfowl areas of North America.

> For further information:
> Website: www.ducks.org
> Address: 1 Waterfowl Way, Memphis, TN 38120
> Telephone: 800-453-8257
> Email: jrich@ducks.org

PICK ONE
WAYS TO VOLUNTEER
(in alphabetical order)

Habitat for Humanity International (HFHI)

Founded in 1976, HFHI is a nonprofit, ecumenical Christian ministry whose goal is decent shelter for everyone, worldwide. The organization utilizes volunteers plus donations of money and materials to build or rehabilitate houses with the help of partner families. Houses are sold to families at no profit, and the monthly mortgage payments are used to build more Habitat houses. Houses are based upon need regardless of background, race, or religion.

Habitat houses are not given free. An affordable down payment and mortgage payments are required. The houses are sold to partner families at no profit and the families invest hundreds of hours building their own houses and also help to build other Habitat houses. The cost of Habitat houses ranges from $800 in some developing countries to an average $60,000 in the U.S.

Selection of families is based on three criteria: level of need, willingness and ability to contribute sweat equity, and ability to repay the loan.

HFHI works through independent, locally run affiliates that direct all aspects of home building, including fundraising, family selection, site selection, construction, and the servicing of mortgages. Local affiliates are asked to give 10% of their received donations for house building in other countries.

HFHI has built more than 300,000 houses in countries around the world, providing decent shelter for some 1.5 million people.

There are a number of HFHI volunteer programs. In the Gulf Recovery program, with the help of tens of thousands of volunteers, more than 1,300 homes have been built or are under construction in Louisiana, Mississippi, Alabama, and Texas.

The Global Village program gives volunteers the opportunity to provide decent housing alongside members of a host community in another culture. And the Women Build program trains women to build houses, and more than 1200 units in various countries have so far been built by all-women crews.

Volunteers of the HFHI Disaster Response program work in the areas of preparedness, mitigation, emergency shelter, and long-term recovery.

For further information:
Website: www.habitat.org
Address: 121 Habitat Street, Americus, GA 31709
Telephone: 800-422-4828
Email: publicinfo@habitat.org

PICK ONE
WAYS TO VOLUNTEER

(in alphabetical order)

Kids Against Hunger (KAH)

Founded in 1999, KAH packages and distributes specially developed, nutritionally complete food packages to hungry children in the U.S. and to starving children in developing countries.

The organization purchases raw ingredients that are specially formulated by food scientists to provide easily digested protein, carbohydrates, and vitamins necessary to prevent malnutrition and hunger-related diseases in children. The food packages are simple to prepare in that they require only boiling water to make a complete meal.

Since its inception, and with the help of more than 100,000 volunteers, KAH has sent some 50 million food meals to children, including a million meals sent to victims of Hurricane Katrina. Shipping is provided either by the U.S. Government or by recipient humanitarian organizations.

Volunteers package ingredients at the main facility in Minnesota and at some 30 independently run satellite facilities in 19 states and one in Canada. The entire network has the capacity to produce more than 20 million meals each year.

In addition to children volunteers (as its name implies), KAH volunteers come from all age groups, and from such organizations as churches, synagogues, schools, social clubs, businesses, senior centers, and civic groups. Volunteers are often composed of a family unit of children, parents, and grandparents. And schools and corporations perform packaging as a community service event.

See the KAH website for specific locations of facilities.

Kids Against Hunger (KAH), continued

For further information:
Website: www.feedingchildren.org
Address: 5401 Boone Avenue N, New Hope,
    MN 55428
Telephone: 866-654-0202
Fax: 763-504-2943
Email: info@kidsagainsthunger.com

PICK ONE
WAYS TO VOLUNTEER
(in alphabetical order)

Kiwanis International (KI)

The name "Kiwanis" derives from the language of a Native American tribe, the Otchipew, who lived in the Detroit area where Kiwanis was originally founded. It is interpreted as having meant either "we trade," "we share," or "we make a noise." And that seemed a useful name for the Kiwanis founders, who wanted to share and, at the same time, "make a noise" or a real difference in the community.

Today, Kiwanis International is a global organization of volunteers with more than 600,000 members in some 13,000 clubs, located in more than 90 countries around the world.

With an emphasis on helping children, volunteers feed the hungry, shelter the homeless, care for the sick, mentor the disadvantaged, build playgrounds and other facilities, and raise funds for medical research.

Members are guided by six "Objects" that are paraphrased here:

- To give preference to human and spiritual values.
- To encourage living in accordance with the Golden Rule.
- To promote the highest social, business and professional standards.
- To develop more effective citizenship.
- To form enduring friendships and build better communities.
- To promote righteousness, justice, patriotism and goodwill.

Kiwanis sponsors a number of youth-oriented service clubs in the U.S. and around the world. K-Kids is for children in elementary schools. Builders Club is for middle school students. Key Club International is the largest service club for high school students in the world and includes some 250,000 member volunteers. Circle

K International, another affiliate, is for college students. And the Aktion Club is for disabled persons.

Kiwanians around the world have a common goal: to serve the children of the world, to create better leaders, and by doing so to build stronger communities.

For further information:
Website: www.kiwanis.org
Address: 3636 Woodview Trace, Indianapolis,
    IN 46268
Telephone: 800-549-2647
Fax: 317-471-8323
Email: foundation@kiwanis,org

PICK ONE
WAYS TO VOLUNTEER
(in alphabetical order)

Lions Clubs International (LCI)

LCI's motto is "we serve," and its volunteers have long been noted worldwide for their service to the blind and visually impaired. Some 1.3 million men and women volunteers in 205 countries conduct vision screenings and support eye hospitals. LCI's SightFirst Program has provided preventive and corrective eye care procedures to literally hundreds of millions of children and adults.

But LCI does a great deal more. The Services for Children Program improves the lives of children and young adolescents in difficult circumstances by providing food, shelter and clothing, medical assistance, drug and alcohol abuse education, immunizations, assistance in coping with disabilities, literacy programs, and vocational training.

The LCI Alert program prepares for potential natural disasters, mad-made disasters and large-scale healthcare crises.

Local clubs do community cleanup, plant trees, and do recycling. Members work to improve schools, renovate nonprofit community centers, repair camps for disabled children, do maintenance on public parks and playgrounds, as well as a host of other community projects.

LCI is making a difference in almost every country in the world. With your help it can do even more.

For further information:
Website: www.lionsclubs.org
Address: 300 W. 22nd St., Oak Brook, IL 60523
Telephone: 630-571-5466
Fax: 630-571-5735
mail: lcifdevelopment@lionsclubs.org

PICK ONE
WAYS TO VOLUNTEER
(in alphabetical order)

Meals on Wheels Association of America (MOWAA)

Local Meals On Wheels (MOW) programs are independent chapters that deliver hot, ready-to-eat meals to homebound persons who cannot provide their own. Recipients include the elderly, sick and disabled persons, and bedridden women with high-risk pregnancies. Some require long-term help while others are only temporary.

Services to elderly, frail individuals often allow them to remain in their homes and avoid being placed in institutions. In addition to delivering meals, this service provides a safety check on the health or other needs of a recipient.

Some local programs suggest voluntary contributions from recipients if they are able, while others charge modest fees. However, eligibility to receive meals is determined solely by medical need, and no one is turned away if they are unable to pay.

The national association, MOWAA, provides funding, technical support, and training for local programs

Limited resources and a growing need are straining the capacity of MOW programs. In particular, programs in rural areas are hard hit because of the times and distances required to make deliveries. MOWAA is developing a national plan, involving corporate, nonprofit, and academic input, to address this problem.

MOWAA has also developed guidelines and training programs for emergency preparedness to enable local MOW workers to respond to events that can disrupt deliveries.

Local MOW programs deliver meals to millions of seniors and other needy persons throughout the U.S. These services would not be possible without the help of tens of thousands of volunteers. Volunteers don't have to be good cooks in order to help, nor do they have to contribute large periods of time. While some volunteers do prepare meals, others package them, deliver them, organize delivery schedules, load vehicles, etc.

For many recipients their only human contact is when meals are delivered. In addition to practical help, volunteer activities that are needed are a smiling face, simple acts of kindness, and perhaps a bit of conversation to a lonely person.

> For further information:
> Website: www.mowaa.org
> Address: 203 S. Union St., Alexandria, VA 22314
> Telephone: 703-548-5558
> Email: mowaa@mowaa.org

Pick One
Ways to Volunteer
(in alphabetical order)

Mercy Ships (MS) (a sectarian organization)

MS has operated a fleet of hospital ships that have provided free medical in developing nations since 1978. The ships include state-of-the-art operating rooms and intensive care facilities. Volunteer crews from more than 30 nations serve onboard.

The organization has performed in excess of 30,000 surgeries (such as cleft lip and palate, cataract removal, facial reconstruction, crossed-eye correction, etc.), 180,000 dental treatments and has treated several hundred thousand people in village medical clinics. MS trains local health-care professionals in modern techniques and has taught some 100,000 people to perform primary health care.

MS has delivered in excess of $60 million of medical equipment and supplies. The organization also has completed hundreds of community projects, including water wells, schools, clinics, and orphanages in more than 70 nations.

More than 850 persons from some 40 nations serve as crews on the organization's ships, and more than 1600 short-term volunteers serve on the ships each year.

The Mercy Teams volunteer program offers short-term opportunities for schools, churches, civic organizations, and groups of individuals to volunteer for operations in both developing and developed countries. All logistics are handled by the organization.

Volunteer projects include renovating orphanages, building clinics, teaching basic health practices, constructing homes, establishing local micro-enterprises, and serving on board ships. There are roles for everyone from carpentry, sewing, painting, providing basic health care, or even simply building friendships with the local people.

NOTE: In addition to its healing and community support services, MS has an active Christian ministry program.

Mercy Ships (MS) (a sectarian organization), continued

For further information:
Website: www.mercyships.org
Address: PO Box 2020, Garden Valley, TX 75771
Telephone: 800-939-7111
Email: mercyteams@mercyships.org

PICK ONE
WAYS TO VOLUNTEER

(in alphabetical order)

Reading Is Fundamental (RIF)

When Margaret McNamara presented the boys she was tutoring a used book and said each boy could keep one, they were delighted. That led to her discovery that none of them had ever owned a book. That was in 1966 in Washington, D.C. and it was the inspiration that formed the organization called Reading Is Fundamental.

That led to book distribution projects in the public schools of Washington, D.C. and spread until, in 1975, the U.S. Congress passed legislation to create the Inexpensive Book Distribution Program. The legislation provided for matching funds for RIF's national book program.

Today, the U.S. Department of Education, several corporations, foundations, and community organizations, with the support of thousands of individual donors and volunteers, all help support RIF's programs. These programs operate in all 50 states plus the District of Columbia, Guam, Puerto Rico, and the U.S. Virgin Islands.

RIF volunteers distribute books to libraries, schools, childcare facilities, domestic shelters, and even migrant camps, focusing especially on children at risk of educational failure.

RIF is now the oldest and largest nonprofit literacy organization in the United States.

Operating at some 21,000 sites, RIF provides five million children with about 17 million free books each year. The organization also offers programs for family literacy and older students mentoring younger children in reading. None of this could be done without the continuing help of volunteers.

More than 450,000 volunteers support the work of RIF. Volunteers help in a number of ways including selecting and ordering books, organizing book events, reading books aloud, conducting sessions to expand reading motivation, generating publicity, holding fundraisers, and helping to obtain in-kind donations from local businesses.

> For further information:
> Website: www.rif.org
> Address: 1825 Connecticut Ave. NW, Suite 400,
>   Washington, DC 20009
> Telephone: 202-536-3400
> Email: development@rif.org